Carol Smith's Customer Relations Series

D1297800

Customer service is one person doing something for one other person—whether that other person is a paying customer, a coworker, or an associate. This Customer Relations Series offers tools and techniques for improving all types of customer relationships. To achieve that goal, this series examines many aspects of homebuilding and remodeling.

Virtually anyone who has contact with customers of any type will benefit from this series. Our audience includes homebuilding firms of all sizes, remodelers, trade contractors, salespeople, suppliers, mortgage professionals, real estate agents, interior designers, architects, engineers, inspectors, and others.

Book topics include all phases of the homebuilding or remodeling relationship: from sales through construction, from delivery through warranty, and from feedback to improvement. We believe that quality management principles apply to the process as well as they do to the product. By listening to customers, defining the ideal, measuring the real and noticing the difference, professionals improve.

Our constant objective is to identify and present a balanced view of customer relations issues, thereby allowing an informed audience to make informed decisions. Many right ways of serving customers exist. The challenge is to identify and excel in the combination that is right for each company or individual. This series intends to help you do just that. Customer relations improves your reputation and results in satisfied customers, referrals, and repeat clients.

Contents

List of Figures

Chapter 1. Written Communications to Customers

Chapter 2. Scheduled Form Letters

Chapter 3. Occasional Letters

Chapter 4. Letters for Difficult Situations and Tough Customers

Chapter 5. Customer Feedback

About the Author and Series Editor

Carol Smith is the leading customer relations expert for home builders. Her 24 years of front-line experience with customers are immediately apparent in her realistic and practical approach. She has performed over 700 buyer orientations, held the posts of superintendent, custom home sales manager, and vice president of customer relations. In 1999 she initiated Customer Relations Professionals (CRP), an international association that provides education and recognition to customer service professionals.

Since 1986 Smith has presented hundreds of educational programs to builders and associates in the United States and abroad, including NAHB's International Builder's Shows, regional conferences, seminars sponsored by the Home Builders Institute (HBI), Custom Builder Symposiums, and Remodelers' Shows. She developed the curriculum for the Home Builders Institute's full-day Customer Service course.

She launched her newsletter, *Home Address* in 1986 and devotes it exclusively to homebuilding service issues. Smith is an award-winning columnist for *Custom Home* magazine and has written dozens of articles for such publications as *Builders Management Journal*, *Premier Homes*, *Building Homes and Profits*, and *Builder* magazine.

She has written five books, all published by Home Builder Press, National Association of Home Builders. She expanded three of her books into the two-volume set, *Customer Relations Handbook for Builders*. She has also written *Homeowner Manual Model for Builders*, *Building Your Home: An Insider's Guide*, and a series of 12 customer service brochures for builders.

Smith has been a licensed Colorado real estate broker since 1988.

Acknowledgements

Reviewers

The following people reviewed the outline and/or all or part of the manuscript for *Dear Homeowner: A Book of Customer Service Letters for Builders:* Sam Bradley, Sam Bradley Homes, Springfield, Missouri; Robert Hankin, Prefab City, Inc., Poughkeepsie, New York; David Jaffe, NAHB Builder Liability and Legal Research; Karen Kotowski, NAHB Builder Education and Conference; Avon Privette, Statesboro Custom Builders, Zebulon, North Carolina; Bob Whitten, Cooper Homes, Inc., Bella Vista, Arkansas; and William Young, NAHB Consumer Affairs.

Book Preparation

Dear Homeowner: A Book of Customer Service Letters for Builders, the second book in Carol Smith's Customer Relations Series, was produced under the general direction of Thomas M. Downs, NAHB Executive Vice President and CEO, in association with NAHB staff members Robert Brown, Staff Vice President, Knowledge Management; Adrienne Ash, Assistant Staff Vice President, Publishing Services; Charlotte McKamy, Publisher; Doris M. Tennyson, Senior Acquisitions Editor and Project Editor; Andrew Schwarz, Director, Sales and Marketing; David Rhodes, Art and Production Director; and Elisa Subin, Production Editor.

Introduction

The benefits of well-written communications with customers range from reinforcing a desired image to establishing a good defense. The homebuilding process has become a swirling sea of details that sometimes threatens to capsize the builder's staff—no wonder many buyers find it intimidating. A company can deliver a sensational home, but if the process was a nightmare, the homeowners may not be in any condition to realize the value they received. The experience is part of a builder's product. Keep your customers comfortable throughout the experience—and beyond it—with good communications. The regular appearance of your company logo in a customer's mail box with relevant information reinforces a desirable image—competent, efficient, and caring. A sense of knowing what is going on builds satisfaction while the company builds the home.

Keeping buyers informed benefits the builder as well. Much has been said and written about aligning buyer expectations. That process requires repetition of information. In addition, consumers have made their desire for involvement clear. Wise builders respond to both needs. Routine communications can update buyers on construction progress, remind them of upcoming events, or confirm appointments or amounts. Providing substantial information prevents surprises. After buyers move in, standard letters can thank them for buying a house from you, remind them of maintenance tasks, offer additional products or services, or invite their referrals.

With time in short supply for customers and staff, a written campaign is sometimes the best way to achieve these goals. You need to respond promptly to complaints and requests and to document your communications with letters, postcards, faxes, or e-mails. You also need to be careful about what you say and how you say it—to be sensitive to what you are putting on paper.

Once a framework of routine letters is in place, keeping customers updated takes little time and produces big benefits. A written chronicle serves you best when it prevents problems and keeps a customer content. But the benefits of written communications—whether by letter, postcard, fax, or e-mail—extend beyond routine events. Many builders have learned that when conflicts arise, communication and documentation are their greatest allies. The need to document details creates more work in the short term. However, in the long term you will be glad you created a thorough paper trail.

Written Communications to Customers

Every communication to customers represents your company and contributes to your image—from advertising through phone calls, from directional signs through warranty work orders, each detail adds to your customers' impressions.[1]

When writing letters, whether to establish form letters to be used again and again or letters addressing unique situations, focus on your purpose, organize your thoughts, and write clearly. Consider which method is appropriate—letter, fax, or e-mail. Use a friendly and business-like tone, adding a personal touch where possible. Send written communications you are proud of, regardless of the circumstances or your purpose.

You are most likely to stay in touch with your customers, both during construction and after they move into their homes if doing so is quick and convenient. Master the use of an efficient and dependable mail-merge system and establish a comprehensive customer database. Once organized so that you can sort (or filter) customers by closing date, community, model, and so on, you have the practical part of an effective written communication system. While you may want to hand address holiday cards, most other mass mailings can be sent with printed labels without offending anyone. By including customer phone numbers in the database, you can also easily update a homeowner directory or name and address cards— a wonderful resource for your staff.

Four Categories of Letters:
■ Scheduled form letters
■ Occasional letters
■ Letters for difficult situations and tough customers
■ Customer feedback postcards, letters, and forms

Purposes

Builders write to customers for many reasons. This book divides the letters into four categories. Chapter 2 includes form letters that mark the progression of the customer-builder relationship. With few exceptions, every customer you sell to should receive each of these letters. This category might include letters to confirm appointments, "thank you for buying from us," "notify you of the closing date," provide a welcome to warranty, or "alert you that your warranty is about to expire."

If you conduct surveys or send seasonal maintenance reminders, they are part of your standard set of letters. Standardized letters address routine events and serve as informational mileposts in the relationship.

Chapter 3 provides an example of correspondence that conveys unique information because it is too complex to trust to verbal discussions alone or because you want a record of having provided the information—or both. This situational- or occasional-letter category includes some standardized letters and forms that address common issues as well as individually composed letters. You send these letters on an as-needed basis. Examples include—

- asking for a final decision on a change order
- calling buyers' attention to use and care information about a selection
- announcing the turnover of common areas and recreational amenities
- responding to customers' concerns about construction of their new homes
- informing homeowners about a new computer system that will assist you in managing warranty requests

Correspondence in Chapter 4 addresses difficult situations or tough customers. Whether the builder initiates these letters or writes them in response to buyers' communications or behaviors, these letters have in common the fact that the builder would rather not be writing them. They address uncomfortable situations that range from mildly annoying to potentially destructive of the customer-builder relationship.

Initiating communications in negative situations can be an advantage. Chapter 4 shows you how you can put rumors to rest, create the best opportunity to present your side of the situation, and allow customers to see you as forthright. When customers fail to comply with agreements or ask for inappropriate services, documenting your response can prevent confusion and avoid the need to reconstruct your answer. The goal in such situations is to retain goodwill if possible while enforcing appropriate boundaries.

Finally, in Chapter 5 you will find cover letters and survey ideas. Having a system for gathering customer reactions can foster improvements in your company. The same database and mail-merge system you establish for routine form letters can serve you well when surveying your customers.

With a mastery of letter writing basics and some insights into faster (and less formal) means of written communications (such as fax and e-mail), written communications can serve your customers and your company. The fast pace of today's world makes personal attention difficult to provide. Written communications can help, and in many cases, turn out to be the best approach.

Method

Before you write anything to a customer, consider the appropriate method to use. Letter, fax, or e-mail? To a large extent, your answer to this question will have to do with the degree of formality, privacy, and permanence you want or need for your message. Avoid the common mistake of always communicating the fastest way. Just because you have a fax machine or you finally learned how to use your new e-mail system does not automatically mean those methods are appropriate.

Ask yourself as well how urgent the information is and which form will work best for the customer. Is a high-quality written record of value? Then a letter might be best. If speed is more important, the fax machine may be your choice. Or if the customer has a hectic schedule and your information can wait quietly until the customer is ready for it, perhaps e-mail will be your choice.[2]

Content

Finding both the time and the right words for your letters can be a challenge. A blank sheet of paper or empty screen intimidates most of us. Clarifying what you want to say and reducing your thoughts to black and white is not always easy. However, once you form a clear concept of what you wish to say, your letter (fax or e-mail) will nearly write itself. If you find yourself struggling with where to start, focus on the question, "What's the point?" The following suggestions may help you get started.

- Jot down your thoughts on scratch paper (or screen).
- Identify the main points.
- Write down the details that support each main point.
- Arrange your points in a logical sequence and add supporting details to each one.
- Stick to the facts. Keep emotions under control.

Frame your material with a brief introduction and a brief conclusion. Rely on standard openings that eliminate blank-page syndrome. "This letter confirms the conversation we had on Tuesday. . . ." Avoid *I, we, my,* or *our* as the first word of your letter. Instead focus on the customers or the situation, not on yourself or your company. Unless you have had several conversations with the customer using his or her first name, stick to Mr., Mrs., or Ms. in the salutation. If you have any doubt about the level of formality to use in the letter, use the more formal wording.

Bring your letter to a conclusion in a businesslike tone. The conclusion can be as simple as inviting the customer to call you with further questions. Remember that customers are less likely to read long, wordy letters. Therefore, whenever possible, stay within the following guidelines.

- Keep your letter to one page.
- Organize paragraphs with two to three sentences.
- Keep sentences, on average, under 20 words.
- Use words of three syllables or less.

After composing the letter, let it rest several hours or overnight (always overnight if it addresses a difficult situation). Later or the next day, reread the letter aloud. Ask yourself—

- Does the letter say what I intended it to?
- Is the meaning clear?
- Are the main points well supported with appropriate details?
- Are facts expressed accurately and logically?
- How would I feel if I received this letter?

Proofreading is the final step. This letter represents your company; it represents you. And it is going to a customer. Keep these proofreading hints in mind.

- Read the letter forward two times to check for correct tone and meaning.
- Read it backward to check for typing errors.
- Ask someone else to read the letter and give you feedback.

To save time, use one letter to communicate to two or more people whenever you can. For instance, you can provide a carbon copy (cc) or a copy machine copy (xc) of the letter to a real estate agent, trade contractor, or managing agent—anyone who needs to know your position in the situation. A copy of every letter you write to a customer should go into the customer's file, but you do not need to list this file copy in the letter.

If you would like to receive documentation from the U.S. Postal Service showing that your letter was mailed and received, several options are available at your local post office. These options include return receipt requested, registered, and delivery confirmation receipt. The standard postal form for addressing overnight or express mail includes the option of an acknowledgement. (For additional information see the U.S. Postal Service Website at www.usps.gov.)

As another resource for your correspondence work, assemble a collection of copies of your standard form letters and examples of favorite letters addressing unique situations. You can quickly become an expert letter writer with the proper tools and support systems available.

Letter →

The letter, sent the old-fashioned way and arriving a few days (or a few weeks) later is the most formal communication and has the best chance of being private. Depending on circumstances you may want to pay the fee for a return receipt. Overnight service through a variety of carriers can assist when speed is critical.

One advantage to a letter is that the slower process of composing and typing (or printing) gives you time to reconsider your comments. This time can be a plus when the situation is emotionally charged. (More than one person has regretted dashing off a snappy retort to a customer and hitting the send button before calming down. For this reason the same kind of care that goes into a letter should also go into a fax or an e-mail.)

With a comfortable working knowledge of the standard parts of letters, you can readily compose them and feel comfortable that they represent your company well. Figure 1.1 shows a simple format called block style—all the parts line up along the left margin. This style is used for all of the letters in this book. An alternative, called semi-block, involves indenting paragraphs in the body of the letter.

FIGURE 1.1 Block Style Letter Format

Heading	Use formal stationery printed with your company's address and logo. If you are using plain paper, type your address and include your company name but not your name. Follow with two or more blank lines before beginning the letter to center the letter vertically on the page.
Date	Insert the date the letter is prepared. Follow with one blank line before the inside address.
Inside Address	Input the name of the person or persons to whom the letter is sent. Include the appropriate form of address (Mr., Mrs., Ms., and so on). Follow with one blank line before the subject line or the salutation if you do not use a subject line.
Subject Line	This optional line alerts the customer to the subject and makes the letter easy to find in the file. If you use a subject line, include one blank line after the subject and before the salutation.
Salutation	Dear Somebody: The punctuation mark that follows the salutation is a colon. Use the recipient's first name if you speak on a first name basis. Insert one blank line between the salutation and body of the letter.
The body will usually be three or more paragraphs: Introduction, main points, and conclusion. Leave one line between paragraphs	The block style is fast and easy to type. All the parts of the letter line up along the left margin. Insert one blank line at the end of your letter, before the close.
Close	Sincerely, Sincerely yours, Very truly yours, Cordially, and so on. The punctuation mark that follows the close is a comma. After the comma, space down four lines for your signature.
Signature	Sign the letter in blue or black ink and the same way your name is typed.
Your Name	Type your name.
Your Title	Add your title.
Enclosure	Use this notation when you are sending something along with the letter (work order, check, drawing, or so on.)
cc:	This notation indicates that you sent a copy of this letter to another individual or entity. Follow the colon with the name—John Smith, Tom's Tubs, or whatever.
CJS/dms	This notation shows the initials in all caps of the person who dictated the letter and in small caps the initials of the person who input the letter. *The last three notations are used as needed and are not part of every letter.*

Fax ➡

Keep in mind that a fax is not private and may pass through several hands before it reaches the intended recipient. Most computer word-processing software packages include fax templates that prompt you for the recipient's information and automatically supply your identifying information, thereby saving you some time. Some systems permit you to fax from your keyboard. (What will they think of next?)

For faxes involving several pages, you need a cover sheet. If you are designing a fax cover page, use one with a minimum of clip art, which takes longer to transmit and print, and small fonts, which may not transmit clearly. Be certain that your fax cover sheet includes your logo, address, accurate fax and phone numbers, especially area codes (which seem to change weekly) as well as your extension number so that the recipient can navigate your voice-mail maze if he or she needs to call you. Your count of the number of pages sent should include the cover page and as a matter of fax etiquette, when you fax more than four or five pages, call first to confirm that your fax will not create a problem on the receiving end. For multiple-page faxes, send them in reverse order so that the customer will receive them in the correct order.

Figure 1.2 shows a cover sheet that contains typical information. The font shown in Figure 1.2 (Comic Sans MS) reflects the informal nature of faxes.

An alternative to a full cover sheet is offered by office supply stores in the form of a small pad of fax notes. Each measures approximately 1.5 inches by 4 inches and gives you a place to fill in the recipient's identifying information as well as your own. When a cover message is unnecessary, this form can save time and paper.

FIGURE 1.2 Fax Cover Sheet

<Logo>
<Company>
<Address>
<City, State, Zip Code>
Phone: <Phone number>
Fax: <Fax number>

fax

To: [Name of recipient]

Fax: [Fax number]

From: [Your name]

Date: [Date]

Pages: [Number of pages faxed, including the cover sheet]

[Your message—clear, concise, and in a readable size font or legible hand writing]

E-Mail

E-mail is the least formal of your choices. Remember though that like a fax, e-mail is not private, especially when you send it to an office computer. Depending on your computer system (and your comprehension of its use) you can add photos from your digital camera (You do have a digital camera, right?) and attach files to e-mail in a matter of seconds (or hours, as in my case). Having the customer's e-mail address in your computer's "address book" makes this a quick and convenient method of communicating—you do not even need to leave your desk.

E-mail systems prompt you for the recipient's name and your subject, and they automatically add the date, time, and your e-mail address. Spell check offers corrections for most typing errors. As with a fax or letter, you can easily send copies to others—assuming they have e-mail. You may find composing off-line works best to prevent accidentally sending a message before you have completed and polished up your remarks. Avoid ALL CAPS, the electronic equivalent of shouting (unless, of course, shouting is your intent—in which case taking a time out might be a better choice than writing to your customer at the moment).

Be sensitive to your customer's level of sophistication and willingness to communicate via e-mail. The immediacy of this method appeals to many customers while others may be intimidated by the entire concept of the Internet. A customer who is uncomfortable or unfamiliar with this method may not discover your message promptly or might zap it into the twilight zone in an effort to print it. Also, once you establish this line of communication, you may find daily notes from the customer, and you must respond promptly to these messages or risk appearing disinterested. E-mail sets a pace that is sometimes difficult to sustain.

2

Scheduled
Form Letters

By establishing a framework of form letters that go to all buyers or homeowners at predetermined points in the relationship, you create informational comfort for your customers. You demonstrate professionalism and control of details, and the steady flow of information and reminders helps your customers avoid surprises.

You may not use every letter in this section; indeed, some of them address the same issue from different directions. Review each letter and determine if it has a place in your overall customer relations program. If you do not currently use letters in this way, prioritize your choices, and develop your written communication system one letter at a time. In this chapter you have 19 letters to consider. Chapter 5, Customer Feedback, offers more ideas for standard correspondence that you may want to add to your routine communication framework.

> **Jobsite Photos**
> Supplementing letters or postcards with photos of the jobsite is truly appreciated when home buyers live outside the region and cannot visit their new homes. Maintain excitement and comfort with thoughtful communication.

In each company the person designated to prepare and send these letters will vary. In many organizations several individuals or departments might each have responsibility for some of the correspondence. (Fortunately, with computer support, these letters take only a little time to prepare and mail.) Some companies have established a Home Buyer Manager position. This individual serves as liaison between the company and the home buyers from the point of contract through closing when warranty service takes over. Therefore one person would oversee the entire process and all communications with assigned buyers.

Either way, some of the appointment confirmation letters might be completed and handed to the buyer in person when the appointment is set. Rather than assume whom that person might be in your company, or attempt to predict what specific title your organization uses, each sample letter is signed simply, [Builder].

Thank You for Selecting [Builder] ➜

Shortly after you accept a deposit and sign a purchase agreement, send a thank-you-for-your-business letter (Figure 2.1) to the buyers. This letter sets a professional tone and offers an opportunity to highlight the next steps in the process. You can also reinforce information about the person the home buyers should contact with questions. Knowing what to expect and where to go with questions helps buyers feel comfortable and instills confidence that their builder has details under control.

If you do not currently use a homeowner manual, you may want to adapt *Homeowner Manual: A Model for Home Builders* published by Home Builder Press, National Association of Home Builders, for this purpose.[3]

FIGURE 2.1 Thank You for Selecting [Builder]

<Date>

<Home Buyer's Name>
<Address>
<City, State, and Zip Code>

Thank You for Selecting [Builder]

Dear <Home Buyer>:

Congratulations on your decision to build a new home. [Builder] is honored that you have selected us as your home builder.

As your sales associate, <sales associate's first and last names> has explained to you, the next steps in this exciting process include finalizing arrangements for financing and making your selections. <Sales associate> can assist you in coordinating appointments. You can also review detailed information about the mortgage application process and the selection process in your *[Builder] Homeowner Manual*.

While you are finalizing your financing and making selections, we will begin the permitting process and schedule trade contractors. Three conditions need to be met in order for us to begin construction. Obtaining a permit is our responsibility; mortgage approval and selections are your responsibility. We will assist you in any way we can with both of these tasks.

Weather permitting, we are normally ready to begin construction of a new home 4 to 6 weeks after signing the purchase agreement. We work with a target delivery date during the early months and will update you about progress. You are also welcome to check the status of your home by contacting <sales associate>.

The purchase of a new home is a decision that represents an investment of your emotions, money, and time. Typically we will ask you to participate in several appointments—mortgage, selections, preconstruction, predrywall, orientation, closing, and warranty. We respect the fact that these appointments require you to interrupt your normal schedule, and we will do everything we can to conduct them efficiently to minimize inconvenience. Each meeting contributes something of value.

As questions come up—and they are inevitable—please contact <sales associate> for assistance. We use a written system in our sales offices to track and document home buyers' questions. This system assures you a timely response and supports our follow through on commitments we make.

We look forward to working with you through the building process and to having your family as a member of the <community> community.

Best wishes,

[Builder]

Mortgage Application Reminder ➜

Purchase agreements commonly use the phrase "time is of the essence." One of the elements for which this essence is critical is in arranging financing. Many builders start construction only after they receive an approval from the buyer's lender.

While some home buyers shop for a new home only after they have been pre-qualified or pre-approved by a lender, many buyers find the home and builder first and then arrange for their mortgage. Few customers pay cash for a new home, and for most buyers applying for a mortgage requires gathering much information. Buyers seldom consider this task to be a fun part of buying a home and some may drag their feet. The following letter (Figure 2.2.) delivers a gentle nudge.

FIGURE 2.2 Mortgage Application Reminder

\<Date\>
\<Home Buyer's Name\>
\<Address\>
\<City, State, and Zip Code\>

Mortgage Reminder

Dear \<Home Buyer\>:

Preparations to begin construction of your new home are underway. We are finalizing the construction schedule and expect to have the building permit in the near future. We are looking forward to building your new home.

Please contact \<sales associate\> with an update on your financial arrangements. As described in your purchase agreement, buyers should apply for a loan within 5 business days of signing the contract and obtain approval within 45 days. So far, your lender has not advised us of your loan approval. If he or she has any questions, \<sales associate\> can assist.

We can confirm the excavation schedule for your new home as soon as we receive written loan approval from your lender. In addition to the information in your purchase agreement and your *[Builder] Homeowner Manual* regarding financing your home, if we can assist you in any way with these arrangements, please let us know.

We are always willing to work with you to expedite this process and get started on your new home.

Sincerely,

[Builder]

Selection Appointment Confirmation ➜

For most buyers the opportunity to select options, finish materials, and colors is one of the reasons they chose to purchase a new home rather than a resale. In recent years, buyer demand for more choices has made the selection process increasingly complex.

Which Way Do I Go?
Providing a diagram with showroom locations and listing addresses, phone numbers, and contacts can be thoughtful additions to the letter in Figure 2.3, and they may save your buyers inconvenience.

While home buyers appreciate the wide variety of choices builders offer, the time they need to finalize selection decisions can easily exceed the builder's deadline. The sooner home buyers get started, the sooner they will complete the process.

Whether you use a formal design center or offer some choices at the sales office and others at suppliers' showrooms, communicating to buyers clearly about this process is vital to timely completion. Some builders ask for all decisions by one deadline, others offer two or more cut-off dates with categories of items assigned to each. Market conditions and the type of product you build will determine your policy on this issue. Whatever your position, describe it in your homeowner manual and remind buyers of it in a clear and friendly letter such as the one that follows (Figure 2.3).

FIGURE 2.3 Selection Appointment Confirmation

<Date>
<Home Buyer's Name>
<Address>
<City, State, and Zip Code>

Selection Appointment

Dear <Home Buyer>:

One of the most enjoyable aspects of purchasing a new home is selecting options, finish materials, and colors. Section 3 of your *[Builder] Homeowner Manual*, New Home Selections, contains hints that may be helpful to you as you make your choices.

Your selection appointment is set for—

<time>, <date>
with <selection coordinator>

<Selection coordinator> will have a copy of your purchase agreement listing items you have already selected. The coordinator will guide your through the remaining decisions and answer any questions you have.

The Selection Center is open from 11 a.m. until 7 p.m., 6 days a week, Tuesday through Sunday. You may want to spend some time there prior to your appointment to consider your choices and create a list of questions. The phone number is <phone number>.

In addition to reviewing the selection hints in your *[Builder] Homeowner Manual*, we suggest you read Chapter 8, Caring for Your Home, prior to making selections. We also have copies of the *Manual* at the Selection Center for your convenience. The information regarding our warranty commitment and your maintenance responsibilities for various materials and items may influence your choices. We want you to make informed decisions.

If you have any questions please contact me or <selection coordinator.>

Sincerely,

[Builder]

Preconstruction Conference Confirmation ➜

The next letter confirms the appointment for a preconstruction conference (Figure 2.4). This meeting is an effective way to prepare buyers for what to expect next, a proven method to minimize surprises—for them and you. Customers appreciate the attention, and they can develop trust and confidence in a climate of open communications.

Four Steps to a Successful Preconstruction Conference:

- Schedule
- Prepare
  - Review the file
  - Strategize
- Host
- Follow up

Five Valuable Preconstruction Topics:

- Events that will extend the schedule
- "Nothing's happening at the house."
- Quality—Builder's regular inspection of work
- Site-visit guidelines
- How to handle questions

The preconstruction conference is usually attended by the sales associate, the superintendent, and the home buyer. These meetings vary in length from 20 minutes to several hours, depending on the home's size and degree of customization. Sending a copy of your printed agenda with your letter is an excellent idea. The agenda helps the buyer understand the scope and importance of the meeting, and it once again reinforces how well organized your operation is.

FIGURE 2.4 Preconstruction Conference Confirmation

<Date>
<Home Buyer's Name>
<Address>
<City, State, and Zip Code>

Preconstruction Conference

Dear <Home Buyer>:

Your new home's building permit, financing, and selections are now in place. Construction is about to begin, and we know you may have many questions. We offer a Preconstruction Conference to provide you an opportunity to meet the superintendent who will be in charge of building the new home and discuss your questions.

This letter confirms our appointment with you for your Preconstruction Conference—

**<time>, date>
at the Sales Office**

<Sales associate> and <superintendent> will both attend. Your real estate agent, <agent name> is welcome to observe although we do not require <him or her> to attend.

The purposes of this meeting are to review the selections you made, answer questions you may have, and provide an overview of the construction process. Unless an error is discovered between the superintendent's specifications for the home and your selection forms, further changes are inappropriate.

You will find a copy of the agenda enclosed for your review. Please allow one hour for this meeting and keep in mind that a site visit is part of our normal procedure— many buyers bring their cameras.

Prior to this meeting, please list any questions you have so that we can address them. You will find information about the construction process in Chapter 4 of your *[Builder] Homeowner Manual*, Construction of Your Home.

If you have any questions please contact me.

Sincerely,

[Builder]
Enclosure

Orientation Dinner Invitation ➜

Because they want the benefits of a preconstruction conference but suffer from a shortage of personnel or time or both, some builders organize monthly group presentations and invite recent buyers. Including a buffet dinner helps to ensure good attendance. The letter in Figure 2.5 shows one way to invite your buyers to this meeting.

Though a detailed review of individual selections is impractical with this approach, these meetings provide the builder with an opportunity to present general information about the product, the building process, and services. In addition to conveying information, these gatherings allow home buyers to get to know the builder's staff and some of their future neighbors.

The agenda typically begins with a buffet and a brief welcome. Dinner is followed by presentations that might include 5 to 10 minutes each by a mortgage loan officer, selections coordinator, superintendent, orientation rep, closing coordinator (or your title company), and the warranty manager.

Are We Creating a Problem?
As with any customer service procedure, both positive and negative effects are possible. Encouraging home buyers to get to know their neighbors can be risky if one customer becomes disgruntled. The communication mechanism you create with this meeting may provide fertile ground for some issue to grow rapidly out of control. However, forthright communications from the start combined with solid performance should forestall most serious problems. And your buyers will get to meet each other eventually anyway.

Allow time for questions. Supply a short outline highlighting the information covered with room for notes. Reference pages in your homeowner manual in this outline to reinforce the importance of the manual and direct the buyers to complete details. The entire meeting should take no more than 2 hours. By preparing your customers for events to come—whether through a preconstruction conference or an orientation dinner—you increase the probability of them enjoying the building process.

FIGURE 2.5 Orientation Dinner Invitation

<Date>
<Home Buyer's Name>
<Address>
<City, State, and Zip Code>

Orientation Dinner Invitation

Dear <Home Buyer>:

As your new home's building permit, financing, and selections become finalized and we near the start of construction, we know you may have many questions.

We offer a New Buyer Orientation Dinner to provide our home buyers an opportunity to hear the answers to their questions and get an overview of the building process. This dinner also gives you a chance to meet more of your future neighbors.

We hope you will join us for the next New Buyer Orientation dinner. It will take place—

<time>; <date>
<location>

In addition to dinner, we will have presentations by a mortgage loan officer, the selections coordinator, the superintendent who will supervise the building of your home, an orientation representative, a title company representative, and our warranty manager. Your sales associate will also attend.

Prior to this meeting, we suggest that you review Section 4 of your *[Builder] Homeowner Manual*, Construction of Your Home, and list any questions you have. Our speakers will remain after the meeting as long as needed to discuss individual questions.

Please RSVP to <name> at <phone number>. We look forward to seeing you.

Sincerely,

[Builder]

Predrywall Tour Confirmation ➜

Builders have discovered that inviting home buyers to tour their new home after the rough mechanical stage and before insulation generates impressive benefits. As with the preconstruction conference or new buyer orientation dinner, customers appreciate the attention.

Won't They Want to Make Changes?
Some builders fear that this meeting will result in the home buyers requesting more changes. If your cut-off point for changes will have passed by the time of this meeting, your homeowner manual and other communications with the buyers should communicate this clearly. When setting the appointment, you can reinforce this point. Finally, realize that if home buyers have thought of a change they want, they are likely to ask for it even if this meeting does not take place.

Knowing they have this tour coming up, many buyers save their questions and ask them all at once. This practice can minimize interruptions of superintendents or sales associates. Some superintendents express their concern that this meeting takes up significant amounts of their time, but buyers will ask their questions. The issue is whether their questioning occurs randomly or in an organized manner, under some control by staff members.

This meeting also provides a chance to confirm that selections are correctly installed up to this point. That extra phone outlet for the home office is easier to move now than after drywall. Nearly every home includes some errors, some questions, and some misunderstandings. With good communications, minor issues are resolved without becoming major issues.

Figure 2.6 offers a letter to confirm this appointment. By now your home buyers are accustomed to your letters; the similar formatting reinforces the degree of control and guidance you are providing. Buyer confidence grows when they can see that a capable person is in charge.

FIGURE 2.6 Predrywall Tour Confirmation

<Date>
<Home Buyer's Name>
<Address>
<City, State, and Zip Code>

Predrywall Tour

Dear <Home Buyer>:

Construction of your new home has progressed through the framing and rough mechanical stages. We are delighted to invite you to tour your home and would like to confirm your appointment

**<time>, <date>
with <superintendent>**

Please meet at your new home and plan to spend approximately 20 to 30 minutes.

<Superintendent> will point out features of our construction methods and answer questions you have. While the time to make further changes has passed, confirmation that we have installed your selections correctly is important to both of us. Please bring your selections forms and change orders with you. Many buyers find them helpful for reference during this tour.

Because of the potentially dangerous nature of construction sites, we remind you of the safe practices listed in your *[Builder] Homeowner Manual*. We also ask that you arrange for the care of young children so that you can attend this meeting alone. Our primary concern is their safety.

We look forward to your visit and to showing you the [Builder] quality that is going into your new home.

Sincerely,

[Builder]

Construction Updates ➜

Many events and circumstances—permitting, weather, labor shortages, material delays, inspectors' schedules, buyer's change orders—make accurate delivery date predictions a challenge for today's builder, especially during the early stages of construction. For help in dealing with completion dates and excusable delays see Chapter 2 of *Contracts and Liability for Builders and Remodelers.*[4]

Some buyers handle this ambiguity better than others. Although all buyers expect and appreciate seeing their builder manage work on their homes efficiently, providing a definite delivery date may be impossible at the beginning. Nothing should prevent a builder from keeping home buyers informed of the status of their homes.

Large corporations can afford the production costs for special cards, perhaps with color graphics, to update buyers when the house has reached key construction points. Smaller operations may not have the resources for elaborate printing, but any company can send a letter (Figure 2.7), postcard, fax, or e-mail. That effort goes a long way toward keeping customers' confidence. It is especially valuable in regions where trade shortages lengthen construction schedules more than anyone involved wants (an area roughly defined as East Coast to West Coast and from Mexico to Canada).

In drafting your letter, postcard, fax, or e-mail be sure what you say in it is consistent with the information on closing set forth in the contract.

FIGURE 2.7 Construction Update

<Date>
<Home Buyer's Name>
<Address>
<City, State, and Zip Code>

Construction Update

Dear <Home Buyer>:

As you know, [Builder] reviews construction schedules on a weekly basis. We have identified several benchmarks in the construction process that help us determine first a target and later a confirmed closing date. We know you are vitally interested in that information and have many details to arrange around the closing date.

Your home has reached the <stage> stage. The current target closing date is between <date> and <date>. This date may move as construction progresses.

When the home reaches cabinet stage, we will set a firm closing date, and give you a minimum of 30 days notice. Until we set a firm closing date, we recommend that you keep all financial and moving arrangements tentative.

We will be happy to discuss any particular details you may need to know about. Please contact me if you have any questions.

Sincerely,

[Builder]

Closing Date Confirmation ➜

At some point the home is far enough along that fewer factors can impose delays, and the builder should commit to a firm delivery date and notify the buyers. The more notice buyers receive the better, ideally a minimum of 45 days, though many companies can give only 30. For buyers who want to lock a loan, close on the sale of their current home, schedule movers, give notice on a rental they occupy, and arrange other details, anything less than 30 days can cause them expense and inconvenience—which they understandably see as the builder's fault. Avoid this situation if at all possible.

How Much?

Insist that your closing agent send buyers a copy of their settlement sheet prior to closing as the Real Estate Settlement Procedures Act. No home buyer needs the panic that comes from not knowing until 2 hours before closing how much money to bring.

The closing date is usually arranged by phone. To prevent last minute surprises, builders—usually working through the sales associate or in some companies through a closing coordinator—should review closing preparation steps with the buyers. Then confirm the details in a letter (Figure 2.8). While time remains to react calmly, remind buyers about such details as insurance, utilities, certified funds, loan contingencies, and resolving last minute questions.

The closing date confirmation letter is a good time to include a Change of Address booklet from the U.S. Postal Service along with other free brochures on moving from insurance companies and moving companies (see also the U.S. Postal Service's Website— www.usps.gov). Home Builder Press publishes, *Moving into Your New Home*, a brochure you can personalize with your business name, address, and phone number.[5]

FIGURE 2.8 Closing Date Confirmation

\<Date\>
\<Home Buyer's Name\>
\<Address\>
\<City, State, and Zip Code\>

Closing Date Confirmation

Dear [Home Buyer]:

This letter is to confirm that your closing appointment has been scheduled for—

\<time\>, \<date\>
\<address\>

If you have any questions, please contact \<name\> at \<phone number\>.

The asterisk on the enclosed map indicates the location for your closing appointment. Parking is available on the north side of the building or 2-hour metered parking can often be found along the street.

The closing process usually takes approximately an hour. In preparing for this important meeting, please include the following items:

❏ Transfer utility services. Phone numbers are listed in your *[Builder] Homeowner Manual* in the sections on closing.

❏ Arrange for evidence of insurance. Your insurance agent will know what is needed. Allow 2 weeks to obtain verification of insurance.

❏ Plan to bring certified funds. The exact amount is usually calculated quite near to the closing date since some items are prorated to that day.

❏ Confirm with your mortgage lender that all loan contingencies are satisfied. If any further documentation is required, be sure to bring that to the closing.

❏ Closing agents have no authority to negotiate for lenders or builders. If you have any remaining questions, work directly with your lender or contact this office to obtain needed answers prior to the closing.

Soon you will be moving into your new home. We look forward to having you join our community.

Sincerely,

[Builder]
Enclosure
cc: \<Closing agent\>

Thank You for Buying →

The excitement of building a new home can be addicting to some buyers. The meetings, decisions, anticipation, and attention create an emotional roller coaster that stops suddenly when money and keys are exchanged at the closing table. Builders need to wean homeowners off the excitement to avoid them developing the "they got our money, now they turn their backs on us" syndrome. You can help this transition occur more easily with a few transition services. This more gradual separation maintains customer satisfaction and reinforces awareness of customer satisfaction with company personnel.

A thank you letter (Figure 2.9) can be one element of a builder's transition service. The cost is small, little staff time is required, and the effect on the buyer is positive. Combine this letter with a couple of other steps such as a visit from the sales associate to deliver a move-in gift or a visit by the superintendent to confirm that orientation items are complete or to complete the Builder-Initiated New Home Warranty Check-Up covered later in this chapter.

FIGURE 2.9 Thank You for Buying

<Date>
<Homeowner's Name>
<Address>
<City, State, and Zip Code>

Thank You for Buying

Dear <Homeowner>:

Several months ago we wrote to thank you for the confidence you had shown in us by selecting <Builder> as your home builder. Now that your new home belongs to you, our sincere hope is that our performance justified your decision.

We value your business and we appreciate the time, emotion, and money you have invested in your home. As you get settled and get to know <community>, our warranty office will stay in touch with you regarding warranty service. It also can assist you with any maintenance questions you may encounter now or in the future.

All of us wish you many years of enjoyment in your new [Builder] home, and again, thank you for your business.

Sincerely,

[Builder]

Welcome to Warranty ➜

Another transition element might be a welcome-to-warranty letter (Figure 2.10), which you mail 1 or 2 days after closing. You also might include a service request form (Figure 2.11) even though your homeowners got copies of this form with their homeowner manual. Notice the three columns at the right on this form. These columns document your warranty representative's decisions about each item. Because the form is printed on no-carbon-required (NCR) paper, you can give the buyer a copy on the spot. For denials of significant items you will want more detailed documentation, but for minor maintenance items, this form can save staff time.

The procedure this letter describes involves making the first warranty appointment with the customers during the homeowner orientation. Knowing they have an appointment (even if it is changed later) has a calming effect on new homeowners. The result is often fewer phone calls to the warranty office during their first weeks in their new home. (An even more aggressive approach is described in the Builder-Initiated New Home Warranty Check-Up later in this chapter.)

Include a brief review of your reporting procedures for emergency and nonemergency items and outline the next routine contact you plan. In addition to reinforcing information homeowners have heard or read before, the letter shows that your company recognizes they've moved in and stands ready to assist them if needed.

Definition of an Emergency

Provide homeowners with a clear definition of emergencies in your homeowner manual:

- total loss of heat
- total loss of electricity
- plumbing leak that requires shutting off the entire water supply
- total loss of water
- total sewer stoppage
- a situation that endangers the occupants or the home

FIGURE 2.10 Welcome to Warranty Letter

<Date>
<Homeowner's Name>
<Address>
<City, State, and Zip Code>

Welcome to Warranty

Dear <Homeowner>:

On behalf of [Builder] I'd like to welcome you to < community> once again. We all hope that your move went well and that you are enjoying your new home.

While we believe that we delivered an excellent home to you, we recognize some items in your home may require follow-up work. Our limited warranty spells out the services we provide in this regard.

We have a tentative appointment with you for a warranty visit at—

<time>, <date>

We will contact you a few days prior to that date to confirm. Meanwhile, if you notice any nonemergency warranty items that need attention, please note them on a warranty service request form for review at that meeting. I am enclosing a copy of that form for your convenience. You also have two of them in your *[Builder] Homeowner Manual*.

Emergencies are rare, but if one occurs please call our warranty office during normal business hours, Monday through Friday, 8 a.m. to 5 p.m. In the event of an after-hours emergency, refer to the Emergency Phone List sticker inside your kitchen cabinet.

You can find complete details about our warranty procedures and guidelines in Chapter 8, Caring for Your Home, in your *[Builder] Homeowner Manual*.

Please feel free to call me if you have any questions. I look forward to working with you in the coming months.

Sincerely yours,

[Builder]
Enclosure

FIGURE 2.11 Warranty Service Request

Warranty Service Request

For your protection and to allow efficient operations, our warranty service system is based on your written report of nonemergency items. Please use this form to notify us of warranty items. Mail to the address shown above. We will contact you to set an inspection appointment. Service appointments are available from 7 a.m. to 4 p.m., Monday through Friday. Thank you for your cooperation.

Name _____   Date_____

Address_____   Community_____

Phones:

    Home _____   Lot no._____

    Work_____   Plan_____

    Work_____   Closing date_____

Service Requested	Service Action*		
	Warranty	Courtesy	Maintenance

Comments

_____

_____

_____

*Warranty or Courtesy indicates Builder will correct. Maintenance indicates a homeowner's responsibility.

_____

Homeowner

Completion of Orientation Items ➜

Obtaining closure on orientation items is vital to homeowner satisfaction, and it creates a challenge for your company. Depending on the volume of homes you build, you may need several methods to confirm the completion of promised work. Builders use phone calls, personal visits, and written systems. Whatever combination your company uses, make certain these items are completed. The impact on buyer satisfaction and your warranty budget can be positive.

The letter that follows offers one method of dealing with the completion of orientation issues (Figure 2.12). You need to be ready to mail it within a few days of the orientation so it becomes one of the first pieces of mail at the new address. An advantage to using a letter is that homeowners who both work may be difficult to reach any other way. Additionally, the homeowners can respond at their convenience and may even walk their home, list in hand, before responding. This possibility means you are more likely to get accurate answers. Avoid assuming that because you do not receive a response that all items are complete.

Finish the List:

- Alert trade contractors and personnel most often needed for orientation items about the upcoming schedule so they can set some time aside to respond.
- Review the list to identify who needs to do work.
- Copy the list for each required person.
- Deliver, fax, or mail the copy to the appropriate people. (Calls are okay, but follow up in writing.) As they complete items, have each sign and date their copy and return it to you.
- Retain the original list, clean and readable, in the file.
- Research the noted issues, provide responses to the homeowners, and document that fact.
- Check on items no less than once a week until they are completed.
- When all items are complete, follow up with the homeowners to confirm that fact.
- Obtain the homeowners' signatures on the original list, sign and date it, add the returned trade contractors' copies, and forward this material to the Warranty Service Department for the house file.

FIGURE 2.12 Completion of Orientation Items

<Date>
<Homeowner's name>
<Address>
<City, State, and Zip Code>

Orientation Items

Dear <Homeowner>:

Your satisfaction with your new home is important to us. Our records indicate that your homeowner orientation list has been completed. We would like your confirmation of that fact. A copy of that list is attached. Please review it and confirm that all items listed have been resolved.

If you believe that we have overlooked any detail from the original list, please note the number of the item in the space below. If all items have been resolved, simply sign the acknowledgement.

Either way, please return this form in the enclosed envelope by—

<date>

Your feedback about our service or your new home helps us improve our business. Please let us hear from you.

Sincerely,

[Builder]
Enclosure

❏ All homeowner's orientation items have been resolved.

❏ The following homeowner's orientation items still need attention. (You need only list the item number.) _____

Comments

_____

_____

_____

_____

_____

_____   _____
Homeowner   Date

Follow Up on Completion of Orientation Items ➜

After a reasonable time, if you do not receive the acknowledgement form from the homeowner indicating that the orientation items are complete, follow up by letter (Figure 2.13) or phone. However, even this "assumption" letter does not guarantee that you will not get a phone call from a screaming homeowner 2 months later.

If you follow up by phone, you still need to confirm in writing that all items have been completed.

FIGURE 2.13 Follow Up on Completion of Orientation Items

<Date>
<Homeowner's name>
<Address>
<City, State, and Zip Code>

Completion of Orientation Items

Dear <Homeowner>:

We have not received a reply from you to our letter of <date> about the completion of your orientation issues. If we do not hear from you by the date listed below we will assume that all items are complete:

<date>

Your feedback about our service or your new home helps us improve our business. Please let us hear from you.

Sincerely,

[Builder]

Builder-Initiated Warranty Check-Up ➜

For years builders told homeowners to send in a warranty list at
30 days. During the 1980s increased demand for quality and service
began to influence that procedure. Now builders who are aggressive
about service actually ask to come to the home and find things to fix.
The letter that follows (Figure 2.14) addresses this procedure and
includes a builder-created checklist (Figure 2.15) of standard items to
inspect during this appointment. (Note that the letters and discussion
of Figures 2.14 to and including 2.17 presume that a builder has a
strong warranty document. For additional information on warranties
and a sample document see David Jaffe, *Warranties and Disclaimers
for Builders.*[6])

Ironically, builders using this approach report less rather than more
warranty work. The positive attitude this step represents so impresses
homeowners that revenge lists become few and far between.
Homeowners who are not angry are more likely to do normal
maintenance items themselves. With shorter warranty lists to screen
and process, the builder can get them completed faster and increase
customer satisfaction still more.

FIGURE 2.14 Builder-Initiated New Home Warranty Check-Up

\<Date\>
\<Homeowner's Name\>
\<Address\>
\<City, State, and Zip Code\>

New Home Warranty Check-Up

Dear \<Homeowner\>:

Getting settled in a new home is exciting and a lot of work. We hope your move went well and that you are enjoying your new home.

We would like to confirm the warranty appointment we made with you during your orientation:

\<time\>, \<date\>

This meeting has three purposes.

❏ We would like to confirm that the home we delivered to you is performing to [Builder's] standards. A copy of the checklist we review is enclosed.

❏ If you have noticed warranty items you believe need attention, we will review them with you and determine if repairs are needed.

❏ We will answer questions you may have about the operation or care of your home.

Please call to confirm or reschedule this warranty check-up. I look forward to hearing from you.

Sincerely yours,

[Builder]
Enclosure

FIGURE 2.15 Sample Warranty Check-Up

Warranty Check-Up

Name _____   Date _____

Address _____   Community_____

Phones:

    Home _____   Lot no._____

    Work _____   Plan_____

    Work _____   Closing Date _____

❏ 60 Days	❏ Year End
❏ Backfill	❏ Patio door lock
❏ Drainage	❏ Garage overhead door
❏ Downspout extensions	❏ Smoke detectors
❏ Concrete flatwork	❏ Furnace filter
❏ Front Door	❏ Interior doors
❏ Lock and deadbolt	❏ Interior trim
❏ Threshold	❏ Cabinets
❏ Weatherstrip	❏ Tile
❏ Doorbell	❏ Caulk
❏ Back Door	❏ Window operation
❏ Lock	❏ Drywall
❏ Threshold	❏ Floor coverings
❏ Weatherstrip	❏ Homeowner's list

Acknowledgement of Warranty Service Request ➜

During busy times (typically late spring and summer), you may take longer to respond to homeowners than normal. No customer likes to feel ignored, especially when the product carries such a high price tag, so at least acknowledge the communication. Let the homeowners know you received their warranty service request by immediately mailing a postcard (Figure 2.16). Quick, easy, and inexpensive, this card relieves some of the pressure on the warranty staff that can result from a seasonal overload. Customers understand a temporary busy spell; they become angry when they hear nothing. This card can prevent that.

The postcard is also useful when the list is short or the items so clearly warranted that you can forego an inspection and issue work orders right away. In such cases the postcard lets the homeowners know you received the list and help is on the way.

FIGURE 2.16 Acknowledgment of Warranty Service Request

Date _____

Dear _____ ,

This postcard is to acknowledge that your Warranty Service Request dated
_____ arrived in our office. Please note the following information:

❏ The items listed are covered by the warranty. We will issue work orders within 3 days.

❏ We will contact you in the next 3 days to arrange an inspection appointment.

❏ The items listed are subject to direct action by the appliance manufacturer. Please
contact _____ at _____ to
schedule service.

Please call me if you need other information at <phone number>. I will be happy to
answer any questions you might have.

_____

[Builder]

Year-End Warranty Check-Up ➜

Fearing that they will receive a list, many builders avoid initiating contact with homeowners at the end of the warranty period and sacrifice an opportunity to impress buyers. The experience of builders who remind homeowners that their warranty is about to expire has been that the year-end work remains the same. Consider sending a year-end letter such as the one in Figure 2.17. Add the one-time repair request (Figure 2.18) to help eliminate repeated requests for drywall and other shrinkage effects.

In addition to positive reaction from homeowners, this year-end contact offers other benefits. By controlling the timing of year-end warranty visits, builders have fewer disagreements with trade contractors about their warranty liability. Warranty staff workload is more predictable. And the arguments with homeowners who forget their warranty expiration dates and attempt to report items several months later drop dramatically.

Another reason to initiate contact at year end is to create the opportunity to confirm that your homeowners are maintaining proper drainage and document the condition of concrete flatwork. Notes (or even photos) on both subjects can be important in resolving later claims. You can also use the checklist in Figure 2.15 for this appointment or you might develop one with different items. The second enclosure referred to in this letter is a copy of a standard warranty request form (Figure 2.11).

Because of the significance of a home purchase buyers expect and deserve a high level of attention. This warranty checklist is one more way to satisfy that expectation—and look good doing so.

FIGURE 2.17 Year-End Warranty Check-Up

<Date>
<Homeowner's Name>
<Address>
<City, State, and Zip Code>

Year-End Warranty Check-Up

Dear <Homeowner>:

More than 10 months have gone by since you closed on your new [Builder] home. We hope you have found your home and the surrounding community to be a pleasant and comfortable place to live.

As you are aware, the Materials and Workmanship portion of your [Builder] Limited Warranty will expire on—

<date>

As we did at 60 days, we ask to schedule a warranty visit near the warranty year's end to check on the performance of the home we built for you.

Besides the items we would like to check, if you have noticed any items that require warranty attention, please fill out the enclosed service request and one-time repair request forms and return them to our office by <date>. For additional information about warranty coverage and our one-time repair service, please refer to Caring for Your Home, in your *[Builder] Homeowner Manual*.

Upon receipt of your request, we will contact you to set an appointment to view items you have listed and answer questions you may have. If you have no items, but would like us to check the home, please call our office to arrange an appointment.

We look forward to hearing from you.

Sincerely yours,

[Builder]
Enclosures

FIGURE 2.18 One-Time Repair Request

One-Time Repair Request

We provide several first-time repairs for your home. Your *[Builder] Homeowner Manual* lists these repairs under individual headings (for instance, Drywall and Grout) in the Caring for Your Home section. We provide this service as a courtesy and to give you an opportunity to observe methods and materials needed for the ongoing maintenance of your home.

Please submit only one One-Time Repair Request. We suggest sending this in near the end of your warranty year to maximize the benefits you receive. Simply complete and mail this form to our office with your year-end warranty list. Thank you for your cooperation.

Name _____   Date _____

Address _____

Phone (h) _____   Phone (w) _____

_____
Homeowner

Comments:

_____

_____

_____

_____

_____

_____

_____

_____

_____

_____

_____

_____

_____

_____

Seasonal Maintenance Reminders ➜

Too often conflict develops between homeowners and builders over maintenance items. In a typical sequence of events, the homeowners report items on a warranty service request. The builder denies action and faces angry customers who then send in list after list to get even. Or the builder provides inappropriate repairs, resents the work and the cost, raises prices to recapture lost funds, and decides customers are all greedy and pushy. Equally undesirable are homeowners who neglect normal maintenance responsibilities; they may have serious problems later and, again, blame the builder. Dissatisfaction and conflict result. Many of these incidents can be prevented with well-planned and well-timed home maintenance reminders. The following examples show one letter for spring (Figure 2.19) and one for fall (Figure 2.20).

FIGURE 2.19 Seasonal Maintenance Reminder: Spring

\<Date\>
\<Homeowner's Name\>
\<Address\>
\<City, State, and Zip Code\>

Spring Maintenance Reminder

Dear \<Homeowner\>:

As spring approaches you can take a few key steps to ensure your home serves you well through the coming months. Please take time to check these items in and around your home and attend to any that need maintenance.

❑ Clean and test smoke alarms.

❑ Test and reset ground fault circuit interrupters (GFCI) breakers.

❑ Change or clean the furnace filter.

❑ Operate the air-conditioning system; if service is needed it is more conveniently arranged before the busiest part of the season arrives.

❑ Adjust registers and confirm that registers and cold-air returns are clear of furniture or draperies.

❑ Make certain the air-conditioner compressor is level and clear of debris.

❑ Turn the humidifier off.

❑ Pour water down the basement floor drain. As drain water evaporates, sewer odors can seep into the house.

❑ Drain sediment from the bottom of the water heater per manufacturer's instructions.

❑ Inspect grout around tile (floor or wall) and touch up.

❑ Wash windows and screens, clean weep holes, and lubricate tracks.

❑ Check caulking, inside and out, and touch up.

❑ Check garage overhead door, tighten bolts as needed, and lubricate springs with motor oil. Have other repairs done by professionals.

❑ Start and adjust sprinkler system. Test exterior faucets for broken pipes.

❑ Clean gutters and confirm that downspouts or splashblocks drain away from the house.

❑ Look for settling of backfill soils and fill in where needed.

❑ Check exterior paint and stain surfaces (especially stained doors) and refinish as needed.

❑ Plan your first barbecue.

If you have questions please refer to Chapter 8, Caring for Your Home, in your *[Builder] Homeowner Manual*, or call our office for information.

Sincerely,

[Builder]

FIGURE 2.20 Seasonal Maintenance Reminder: Winter

<Date>
<Homeowner's Name>
<Address>
<City, State, and Zip Code>

Winter Maintenance Reminder

Dear <Homeowner>:

As colder weather approaches you can take a few key steps to ensure your home serves you well through the coming months. Please take time to check these items in and around your home and attend to any that need maintenance.

❏ Clean and test smoke alarms.

❏ Test and reset ground fault circuit interrupters (GFCI) breakers.

❏ Change or clean the furnace filter.

❏ Operate the heating system.

❏ Adjust registers and confirm that cold air returns are clear of furniture or draperies.

❏ Clean the humidifier per manufacturer's instructions.

❏ Adjust or replace weatherstripping on exterior doors as needed.

❏ Check the fit of exterior doors; thresholds are adjustable—use a quarter to turn the screws.

❏ Check caulking, inside and out, and touch up.

❏ Drain your sprinkler system.

❏ Remove hoses from exterior faucets. "Freeze proof" faucets will suffer a broken water line if the water in the hose freezes and expands into the pipe.

❏ Inspect chimney for nests.

❏ Review safe fireplace operation. Provide professional cleaning at regular intervals.

❏ Check garage overhead door, tighten bolts as needed, and lubricate springs with motor oil. Have other repairs done by professionals.

❏ Clean gutters, check downspouts; confirm that splashblocks drain away from the house.

❏ Check foundation, concrete, and yard for settling; fill in as needed for positive drainage.

❏ After snowfall, brush snow off gutters and away from downspouts.

❏ Remove ice and snow from concrete as soon as possible; avoid using de-icing agents with damaging salts.

❏ On pleasant days, open windows to allow house to breathe.

❏ Decorate safely for the holidays. Do not overload circuits or use worn extension cords.

If you have questions please refer to your *[Builder] Homeowner Manual*, Chapter 8, Caring for Your Home, or call our office for information.

Sincerely,

[Builder]

3

Occasional Letters

Veterans of the homebuilding industry will be quick to tell you never to say, "Now I've heard it all" because making this statement aloud guarantees something even more astounding will occur shortly. Hundreds of events occur when working with home buyers. Form letters cannot address all of these situations. The various letters that follow by no means address every conceivable customer issue you will ever face. However, many of the situations are common, and you may find you can change a few words or a couple of sentences and produce a letter to serve your particular purpose.

Please notice as you review the samples that follow that each letter strives for a friendly tone, even when patience is running low and frustration is running high. Recognize that while the customer may not always be right, the customer is always the customer, and he or she deserves to be treated with courtesy.

Finalize Selections ➜

Most purchase agreements obligate home buyers to complete the selection process within a specified time frame. Once that deadline passes, the builder faces several choices, all unpleasant ones.

Wait. This choice is frustrating, especially when the same home buyers who are late with selections complain about "late" delivery of the home.

Proceed without all selections. This choice is risky—a potential source of future expense, conflict, or buyer disappointment.

Put the home buyers on notice. This choice might require telling the homeowners that they are in breach of their contract. While this choice may produce the desired result, buyers usually do not take such legal notices well and the unpleasantness might escalate.

The irony of this situation is that builders do everything in their power to meet the original closing date in spite of the buyers' delayed selections. Builders do so because they want to maintain their scheduling positions with trade contractors and collect the expected income revenue from the sale.

Whether indecision, busy schedules, or financial concerns are the cause of the delay, your goal is the same—to get the information you need to order materials and schedule construction of the home and still maintain goodwill. The following letter (Figure 3.1) may help. In addition to mailing this letter, fax it, call, and e-mail the information. Keep a log of all your efforts in the contract file.

Why Are Customers Late?

- Review your expectations. Is the time you allow reasonable for the number of decisions your buyers will need to make?
- Check your contract documents. Do they define the repercussions of late selections?
- Was the information buyers needed to make their choices readily available?
- Were buyers prepared for the number of decisions needed?
- Do you provide browsing time so buyers can consider combinations without taking staff time?
- Are appointments with selection staff long enough?
- Financial constraints may mean that buyers will prolong the process in hopes they can raise the money.

If 1 buyer out of 30 is late your procedures are probably acceptable. If 28 out of 30 miss the deadline, consider some adjustments in your procedures and schedule.

FIGURE 3.1 Finalize Selections

<Date>
<Home Buyer's Name>
<Address>
<City, State, and Zip Code>

Finalize Selections

Dear <Home Buyer>:

Construction of your new home has progressed to the <home's current construction stage> stage. We hope you are pleased with the work done so far.

However, to continue work on your home beyond <date>, we need your decisions on the remaining selections.

Rather than install items that may need to be removed later or that compromise the efficiency of the construction schedule by having trade contractors work out of their normal sequence, we can place your home on hold and stop work pending our receipt of the rest of your selections.

We understand that buyers sometimes need a little extra time to make all their choices. To forestall any disappointment or surprise on your part, we remind you that these additional days extend the total time to complete your home and thus extend the delivery date. Often such an extension is a significant one because of the lead time to obtain some materials and reschedule the affected trade contractors. We also remind you that we charge construction loan interest for selection delays beginning on the third day. These costs are charged at closing. Details are described in <paragraph number> of your purchase agreement.

We hope to help you to avoid these repercussions. Please meet with <selection coordinator> by <date> to complete your selections.

If you have any questions, please contact me.

Sincerely,

[Builder]
cc: <Superintendent>

Highlight Use and Care ➜

If products such as marble, hardwood floors, or brass have caused conflicts with previous buyers, ask future buyers to read and sign information from your homeowner manual about these products. Pulling that material out and focusing attention on it can prevent disagreements later (Figure 3.2). Present a balanced view. Mention good points along with potential concerns and long-term maintenance tasks. "We want you to make informed decisions" is one positive way to present such information.

FIGURE 3.2 Highlight Use and Care

<Date>
<Home Buyer's Name>
<Address>
<City, State, and Zip Code>

Use and Care of Hardwood Floors

Dear <Home Buyer>:

The warmth and ambiance of wood floors add something special to any decor. However, wood floors are not impervious to normal wear, and we want you to know what to expect before making this choice for your home. Please review the following information and keep in mind that preventive maintenance is the primary goal in caring for hardwood floors.

Cleaning. Sweep on a daily basis or as needed. Never wet-mop a hardwood floor. Excessive water causes wood to expand, possibly damaging the floor. When polyurethane finishes become soiled, damp-mop with a mixture of one cup vinegar to one gallon of warm water. When damp-mopping, remove all excess water from the mop. Check with the hardwood flooring company for cleaning recommendations if your floor has a water-based finish.

Dimples. Heavy furniture or dropping heavy or sharp objects can cause dimples.

Filmy Appearance. A white, filmy appearance results from moisture, often from wet shoes or boots.

Furniture Legs. Install proper floor protectors on furniture used on hardwood floors. Protectors will allow chairs to move easily over the floor with less scuffing. Clean the protectors on a regular basis to remove any grit that may accumulate.

Humidity. Wood floors respond noticeably to changes in humidity in your home, especially during winter months when the heat is on. A humidifier helps but does not eliminate this reaction.

Mats and Area Rugs. Use protective mats at the exterior doors to help prevent sand and grit from getting on the floor. These substances are wood flooring's worst enemy. However, be aware that rubber backing on area rugs or mats can cause yellowing and warping of the floor surface.

Recoat. If your floors have a polyurethane finish, in 6 months to 1 year you may want to have an extra coat of polyurethane applied. This extra coat should be done by a qualified contractor. The exact timing will depend on your particular lifestyle. If another finish was used, please refer to the manufacturer's recommendations.

Separation (see also, *Warping*). Expect some shrinkage around heat vents or any heat producing appliances.

Shoes. Keep high heels in good repair. Heels that have lost their protective cap (thus exposing the fastening nail) will mark your wood floor. They will exert thousands of pounds of pressure per square inch on the floor.

Spills. Clean up food spills immediately with a dry cloth. Use a vinegar and warm water solution for tough food spills.

FIGURE 3.2 *(Continued)*

Splinters. While floors are new, small splinters of wood can appear.

Traffic Paths. A dulling of the finish in heavy traffic areas is likely.

Warping. Warping will occur if the floor becomes wet repeatedly or is thoroughly soaked even one time. Slight warping in the area of heat vents or heat producing appliances is also typical.

Wax. Waxing and oil-based products are neither necessary nor recommended. Once you wax a polyurethane finish floor, recoating is difficult because the new finish will not bond to the wax. The preferred maintenance is preventive cleaning and recoating annually or as needed to maintain the desired level of luster.

Sincerely,

[Builder]

I (we) have read the information regarding care and performance of wood floors. We accept the responsibilities that come with the beauty of wood floors.

_____	_____
Purchaser	Date

_____	_____
Purchaser	Date

Release ➜

Buyers sometimes have their hearts set on materials or colors that builders know can cause problems later. Every company has its own pet headaches. To allow buyers the choices they want but ensure that they realize the risks or maintenance responsibilities such choices create, ask buyers to sign a release. Explain the vulnerability of the material, the long-term risks, and the limitations on your liability. Figure 3.3 shows an example of a release for custom stain or paint colors.

FIGURE 3.3 Release for Custom Paint and Stain Mixes

<Date>
<Home Buyer's Name>
<Address>
<City, State, and Zip Code>

Release for Custom Paint or Stain Mixes

Dear <Home Buyer>:

From time to time our buyers ask us to use custom-mixed paint or stain in their new homes. We are happy to accommodate such requests. However, we want to make you aware of the conditions that can result from your selection of custom-mixed paint or stain.

1. Just as dye lots vary in carpet and wallpaper, paint and stain mixes vary based on many factors, including the operator who prepares the mixtures and even which tinter he or she uses.

2. After application, the finished (dry) appearance can look different from what was expected: warm versus cool, red versus gold, light versus dark, and so on.

3. Normal touch-ups can be difficult, if not impossible, to match—whether the touch-up is applied by you or us. Exact matches are unlikely, touch-ups will be readily visible. Likewise, standard surface repair products (such as wood fillers) may not match as well as they do with standard materials.

4. Normal pricing is based on our performing touch-ups as needed prior to delivery. If you prefer that we repaint or restain corner to corner instead of touching up, we will schedule this extra application upon receipt of your payment for this additional work. The cost is based on time and materials, and we quote each job individually.

By selecting custom-mixed paint or stain, you accept responsibility for the conditions described above. Your signature indicates you understand and accept these terms and conditions.

Sincerely,

[Builder]

_____   _____
Purchaser   Date

_____   _____
Purchaser   Date

Finalize Change Orders ➔

As to what causes the most consternation in the construction industry, late selections and unsigned change orders are in close competition. Installing a change without the buyer's signature can be a costly error. More than one builder has heard the words, "Well I won't make you take it out, but I'm certainly not paying for it." Verbal approvals are difficult to collect on at the closing table.

Builders create another vulnerability when they accept change orders so late in the process that the information arrives in the field after the original work is complete. An Omaha builder accepted a late change order and ended up paying twice for carpet—the beige the buyers originally selected and the gray the company permitted them to change to at the last minute.

Establish reasonable change order cut-off dates and enforce them fairly. Back up the cutoff dates with detailed tracking. (Notice how much information the letter in Figure 3.4 includes.) Make it your policy to require signatures and payment (or approval for a higher mortgage amount from the lender) before you accept and install a change.

> **Additional Resource**
> For more information on managing change orders and contract logs see *Sales Management Tool Kit* by Dennis Radice.[7]

Consider adding an expiration date to your change order form (as trade contractors do on their bids). The change order would state: "Unless the change order is signed and paid by <date>, it is null and void, will not be installed in the home, and will not be charged to the purchasers." The Finalize Change Order letter (Figure 3.4) references an enclosed change order (Figure 3.5) that includes this statement.

With a good system, you can afford to be pleasant when a change order lingers without a final decision. By staying on top of open questions such as an unsigned change order, you can start to communicate with the buyers before conditions reach the critical stage in the field. The extra work up front prevents much unpleasantness later and allows your field personnel to build homes in an orderly manner.

FIGURE 3.4 Finalize Change Order

<Date>
<Home Buyer's Name>
<Address>
<City, State, and Zip Code>

Finalize Change Order

Dear <Home Buyer>:

On <date> you requested pricing on custom change order number <number of change order>. A copy is enclosed for your reference.

Our purchasing manager, <name>, completed the pricing and forwarded the information to <sales associate> on <date>. When <he or she> informed you of the price by phone and fax on the same date, your response was that you wanted to think it over for a couple of days.

Our goal is to build your home with the features you want. To do so we need your help. We now need your response to this change order by—

<date>

This change order expires on this date. After this date, construction of your home will proceed without this change.

As outlined in <paragraph number> of your purchase agreement, we require your signature and full payment to incorporate a change order into your home. Please contact <sales associate> with your final decision or any questions you have.

Sincerely,

[Builder]
Enclosure
cc: <Sales Associate>

FIGURE 3.5 Change Order

Change Order No. _____

Purchasers _____ Date _____

Contract Dated _____ Plan_____

Address_____ Lot no. _____

Description of Change Requested

_____

_____

_____

_____

_____

_____

Administrative fee $ _____   Drawing attached _____

Cost of change $ _____   Delivery date adjustment _____ days

Credit (deleted items) $ _____   Expiration date _____

     Total $_____

The change described above, its cost, and the corresponding adjustment in the construction schedule have been requested by Purchasers. By signing this Change Order, Purchasers agree to pay for this change and acknowledge that the estimated delivery date for the home is revised accordingly. [Builder] will incorporate the change into the home only if the requested change described has been approved and signed by [Builder], and signed and paid in full by Purchasers prior to the expiration date above. Once the expiration date has passed, [Builder] has the options of changing the cost and delivery date adjustment, or declaring the change requested null and void.

_____   _____

Approved   [Builder]   Date

_____   _____

Purchaser   Date

_____   _____

Purchaser   Date

Buyer Wants to Know Response →

The excitement (or in some cases paranoia) of watching the new home go up is part of what builders sell. Site visits and associated questions or lists from buyers are inevitable. An effective system for accepting and responding to these questions combined with a healthy respect for the home buyers' right to ask go a long way toward preventing serious problems during construction.

Determine to whom buyers should direct their questions and in what form. A written system eliminates much confusion and provides your personnel with a place to record their responses. For many companies the sales associate handles this task. Some organizations have created positions with titles such as Home Buyer Manager to serve as customer liaison once the contract is signed. This person oversees setting standard appointments, gets change orders approved and signed, and answers questions during construction.

The goals are to—

- be responsive to customer concerns

- correct errors that occur in the field (Buyers sometimes find important items that save builders money.)

- allow the superintendent to proceed with as few interruptions as possible

- establish a paper trail of issues that arise

A standardized system to document buyers' questions and your responses can make this process routine, save time, and accomplish all of your goals. The letter in Figure 3.6 shows possible responses to a buyer's questions that a sales associate received on a Buyer Wants to Know form (Figure 3.7).

Not all buyers' questions require a letter; minor items can be handled in conversation ("When will my shutters be installed?" "Next week," requires no documentation). But responses to significant items are best documented with a letter. ("You've installed the wrong color carpet.") The time you take to work within such a system is more than returned to you by the conflicts you prevent.

FIGURE 3.6 Buyer Wants to Know Response

\<Date
\<Home Buyer's Name>
\<Address>
\<City, State, and Zip Code>

Buyer Wants to Know Response

Dear \<Home Buyer>:

Thank you for your Buyer Wants to Know form, dated \<date> and requesting information on three items. You will find a copy enclosed for your convenience. We have investigated your concerns.

Item 1, \<Name of superintendent>, your superintendent confirmed to us that this item is scheduled to be completed or corrected on \<date>.

Item 2 is correctly installed as your selection sheet ordered. If you wish to make a change, please see your sales associate no later than \<date>, the final date such a change will be possible without additional costs and extension of the construction schedule.

Item 3 has been installed in accordance with the specifications for your house. The specifications are \<exhibit> of your contract. If you wish to make a change, please see your sales associate no later than \<date>, the final date such a change will be possible without additional costs and extension of the construction schedule.

If you have any questions about any of these items, please contact me.

Sincerely,

[Builder]
Enclosure

FIGURE 3.7 Buyer Wants to Know Form

Date _____

Lot no. _____

Our Buyer Wants to Know . . .

_____

_____

_____

_____

_____

_____

_____

_____

_____

_____

_____

_____

_____

Customer _____ Phone_____

Please provide the requested information to the sales office by <date>.

<Sales Associate>

Response

_____

_____

_____

_____

_____

By _____

Response forwarded to customer on _____ ❏ Phone ❏ Letter ❏ In person

By _____

Closing Bulletin ➜

"Ghosting"—the accumulation of a grimy film along the edges of carpets, under doors, on walls around switch plates and outlets, and on other surfaces of a home provides an example of a new situation builders must address. The response provides a model for any new information builders need to convey to buyers already under contract.

Appropriate long-term steps include informing future buyers through the homeowner manual and a discussion of ghosting at their orientation. But what about buyers already under contract and waiting to close—who have already received a homeowner manual without the new entry? They will hear the information at their orientation, but you will have no proof of that without something in writing.

A temporary notification—delivered, explained, and signed at closing—ensures that no one misses getting this important information. Provide this information to buyers at closing until you begin closing with buyers who received the information as part of your homeowner manual. The example in Figure 3.8 addresses ghosting, but the technique can work with many subjects.

FIGURE 3.8 Closing Bulletin

Attention Home Buyers!

Recent feedback from homeowners (in both old and new homes) regarding black sooty stains that develop on surfaces in homes (carpet, walls, ceilings, appliances, mirrors, and around area rugs—to list a few examples) have caused much investigation and research.

The conclusion of research and laboratory tests has been that the majority of this staining or "ghosting" results from pollution of the air in the home caused by burning scented candles. Incomplete combustion of hydrocarbons as these candles burn contributes a considerable amount of soot to the air. This sooty substance then settles or accumulates on surfaces in the home. These deposits are extremely difficult to remove. On some surfaces (light colored carpet, for instance), they can be impossible to clean completely away.

The popularity of scented candles has increased many fold in recent years. If this activity is part of your lifestyle, we caution you about the potential damage to your home. When this condition results from homeowners burning candles or making other lifestyle choices, the resulting damage is excluded from our limited warranty coverage.

_____   _____

Acknowledged   <Purchaser>   Date

_____   _____

<Purchaser>   Date

Information Bulletin →

Neighborhood news, developer events, or community or homeowners' association updates are a few of the categories that may generate a need for a builder to communicate to home buyers and homeowners. In some cases, as shown in the sample in Figure 3.9, one letter may update customers on more than one issue. Think of this approach as a quick newsletter to your customers. (Large homeowners' associations take over this function once they are established.) At times, one letter may be appropriate for your buyers with a slightly different version for homeowners.

Remember, especially if the news is unpleasant—the pool construction has been delayed until next year—you are generally better off in the long term if you volunteer facts rather than allow rumors to circulate. Mentioning a subject first allows you to set the tone.

FIGURE 3.9 Information Bulletin

<Date>
<Home Buyer's or Homeowner's Name>
<Address>
<City, State, and Zip Code>

Information Bulletin

Dear <Home Buyer or Homeowner>:

This bulletin is a good-news, bad-news letter.

The Good News—The tennis courts planned for <Community> are scheduled to open <date>. Use of the courts this summer will be on a first-come, first-served basis. By next season the <Community> Homeowners' Association (HOA) Recreation Committee will be operating, and they will establish a sign-up system.

If you are interested in serving on the Recreation Committee or any other HOA committee please contact <name> for information.

More Good News—The final paving of the main street is scheduled for <date> with a rain date of <date>. At that time signs will be posted and traffic will be rerouted until the work is complete.

And the Bad News—We have had to postpone the installation of the permanent entry lights by several weeks. The city is reviewing the plan because of the new design, and until we have final approval, we cannot perform this work. We expect approval by the end of next month and have tentatively rescheduled installation for the week of <date>.

All of us look forward to having these items completed. We will provide additional updates as appropriate. If you have any questions, please contact me.

Sincerely,

[Builder]

Aftermath of Severe Weather ➜

When storms (or any natural disaster) strike, homeowners may assume their builder will repair any damage. The underlying expectation is that a new home should be built to withstand nature's best efforts. When requests for storm repairs come in, you are left with two choices: provide the repairs or advise the homeowners to contact their insurance carriers. The latter advice may lead to disagreements—sometimes serious—with your customers.

As mentioned earlier, being the first party to raise a subject has some advantages. With a standard letter ready to go, a mass mailing reminding homeowners of the responsibility of their insurance carriers can dramatically reduce the phone calls to (and arguments with) your warranty office. (Similarly, as the season for freezing temperatures approaches, a reminder to homeowners to drain their sprinkler systems and remove exterior hoses can eliminate many problems.)

Imagine that a severe windstorm hits your area. Within 24 hours your database prints labels for all homeowners, and you mail out suggestions (Figure 3.10) on what homeowners should do. If phone calls come in, your staff has a positive response. "Yes, Mr. Jones, that was a terrible storm. In fact we are mailing our homeowners guidelines on how to proceed. May I fax you a copy right now?" This response is better than a heavy sigh, and "No, we do not cover storm damage. Your insurance company should handle that."

Back up this response with a willingness to inspect any damage that the homeowner's insurance company claims resulted from faulty materials or construction practices. Your goal is not to sidestep your responsibilities, but to put appropriate damage claims on the shoulders of the insurance companies.

FIGURE 3.10 Aftermath of Severe Weather

\<Date\>
\<Homeowner's Name\>
\<Address\>
\<City, State, and Zip Code\>

Severe Weather Reminder

Dear \<Homeowner\>:

Yesterday's storm was severe and according to news reports caused significant damage to trees and homes in our area.

We suggest that you promptly inspect your property and report any damage you find to your homeowner's insurance company. Look for pieces of shingles in your yard or gutters, broken tree limbs, damaged fencing, or other effects of the storm.

Photographs help document such damage and may support your claim. Although storm damage is excluded from our limited warranty coverage, if you need information on how to prevent additional damage while you await an inspection and response from your insurance company, we may be able to make preventative suggestions.

If you have questions, please contact me.

Sincerely,

[Builder]

Explanation of Policy or Procedure →

Whether you have changed processing methods—perhaps because of new computer software—or want to reinforce established procedures, a written approach can work well. It also is your easiest way to communicate with all of your customers.

When you are announcing changes, as shown in Figure 3.11, call attention to the benefits your customers receive from the change. Then describe the new procedure clearly. When you are reinforcing established procedures as in Figures 3.12, 3.13, and 3.14, keep your tone friendly and invite customers to contact you with questions. Although none of these policies should be a surprise to homeowners because they are explained in your homeowner manual and discussed at the homeowner orientation, expect to review them with a few homeowners. Some will test your commitment to established systems, others simply did not absorb the information. Either way, courtesy is in order.

FIGURE 3.11 New Warranty Procedure

<Date>
<Homeowner's Name>
<Address>
<City, State, and Zip Code>

New Warranty Procedure

Dear <Homeowner>:

On <date> we converted to a new computer system to track our warranty work. Now that we have rounded the learning curve, we look forward to using this new system to serve you faster and more accurately as well as to provide excellent documentation.

We know you expect a quick response when you need warranty attention. Logging warranty items into the new system is simpler and faster than with our previous system. The new program also allows us to monitor completions and feedback. Improved communications to our trade contractors will help them help you. And you will now receive a copy of all work orders issued for your home.

Your cooperation in using the new system will make it work even better. The system is based on your written report of nonemergency items. This system protects you by documenting all items for your permanent file, and it allows our staff to focus on producing results for you as efficiently as possible. If an inspection of an item is necessary, we will contact you to arrange a time.

You are welcome to report nonemergency items by mail, fax, e-mail, or you can drop your list off in person at our main office during normal working hours, 8:30 a.m. until 5 p.m., Monday through Friday. For after-hours drop off, please use the slot in the door.

Please note that the procedure for reporting an emergency has not changed. During our business hours (8:30 a.m. to 5 p.m., Monday through Friday), please call our office <phone number>. Outside of those hours, please refer to the emergency phone sticker we installed on the inside of a kitchen cabinet door.

If you have any questions, please contact me.

Sincerely,

[Builder]

FIGURE 3.12 Service Hours

<Date>
<Homeowner's Name>
<Address>
<City, State, and Zip Code>

Service Hours

Dear <Homeowner>:

Routine monitoring of work orders has called our attention to warranty work for your home that remains incomplete.

Work Order No.	Trade Contractor	Phone No.
<Number>	<Trade Contractor's Name>	<Trade Contractor's Phone No.>
<Number>	<Trade Contractor's Name>	<Trade Contractor's Phone No.>

We are committed to providing you with effective service under the terms of our warranty. Appointments for warranty work are available between the hours of 8 a.m. and 4 p.m., Monday through Friday.

Please call our office or the trade contractors listed above to set up a service appointment.

If the service hours are inconvenient for you at the present time, we will be happy to place the service orders on hold for up to 30 days or until you notify us to re-activate them, whichever comes first.

If you wish to exercise this option, please call our office at <phone number> to let us know.

Sincerely,

[Builder]
cc: <Trade contractors listed>

FIGURE 3.13 Method of Repair

\<Date\>
\<Homeowner's Name\>
\<Address\>
\<City, State, and Zip Code\>

Method of Repair

Dear \<Homeowner\>:

In response to your request, we issued work order number \<work order number\> on \<date\>.

The work order provides for repair of \<item\>. This repair has been performed in the past with excellent results.

According to the terms of the limited warranty, the choice of a method of repair is specifically the company's. You do have the option of taking responsibility for correcting the item at your own expense and using a method of your choice. If you prefer to use another method of repair, simply inform the service technician or trade contractor. We will cancel the work order and consider this matter resolved.

The service technician or trade contractor assigned to complete this work will contact you during the next several days to arrange an appointment during normal service hours (8 a.m. to 4 p.m., Monday through Friday).

Please call me if you want to discuss this work order or if you have any concerns about the intended work or our procedures.

Sincerely,

[Builder]
cc: \<Service technician or trade contractor\>

FIGURE 3.14 Check Instead of Repair

<Date>
<Homeowner's Name>
<Address>
<City, State, and Zip Code>

Check Instead of Repair

Dear <Homeowner>:

Work order number <work order number> was issued on <date> for warranty work needed in your home. Several attempts to provide the work listed have been unsuccessful.

After three appointments have been set without obtaining access to a home to provide a repair, our policies provide us the option of paying you for the work indicated. You may then schedule the repair at your convenience and with a repairperson of your choice.

You will find enclosed check number <check number> to pay for the repair of the item listed on work order number <work order number>. The amount of the check is based on the cost to [Builder] for performing the work listed on this work order. We have voided the work order and recorded this item as resolved in your file.

If we can provide you with any information that will assist you in having this work performed, please feel free to call me.

Sincerely,

[Builder]
Enclosure
cc: <Service technician or trade contractor>

Turnover of Common Areas to a Homeowners' Association ➜

The turnover of common areas to a homeowners' association is a significant turning point in a builder's relationship with a community. The builder looks forward to this separation, and usually the homeowners' association resists it.

A deliberate strategy for managing this rite of passage helps. Knowing how you will manage these transitions permits you to prepare the buyers for the turnover. Develop a clear overview of your procedures and deliver it to buyers with other association documents. Behind the scenes, include a discretionary amount in your budget from the beginning so that you will be prepared to provide something extra.

In your planning, compile a checklist of common area items to inspect—sod, shrubs, trees, sprinkler systems, post lamps, concrete flatwork, rock walls, and so on. Support the list with appropriate standards. Set a timely appointment to conduct a homeowners' association orientation on the common areas with no more than three association representatives and at least two company people. Invite appropriate trade representatives—sprinkler, swimming pool, and so on. Review proper use and maintenance of each component, turn over any manufacturers' literature, and identify items you should correct. Provide the association representatives with a copy of the list you compile.

Make this list a top priority and promptly complete each item you listed. Avoid band-aid approaches; fix problems properly. During the common area orientation, the association will undoubtedly ask for something extra. Use your discretionary budget amount to be a hero and pleasantly make a point of the gift. Upon completion of all items to be corrected, send a letter similar to Figure 3.15 with a copy to all affected homeowners.

FIGURE 3.15 Turnover of Common Areas

<Date>
<Homeowners' Association>
<Address>
<City, State, and Zip Code>

Turnover of Common Areas

Dear <Board of Directors>:

Congratulations! The common areas at <Community> are now under the control and care of the <Community> Homeowners' Association.

The list we created during our tour of the common areas on <date> is now complete. Maintenance of these areas and all amenities they contain are now an Association responsibility.

In addition, as you requested, <Builder> purchased and installed two trees in the entry island and added more ground lighting for the entry signs. The results are beautiful, especially at night. We are pleased to present these items to the Association as a gift.

All information, warranties, instruction manuals, and suppliers' and trade contractors' names, addresses, and phone numbers have previously been turned over to the Association. <Swimming Pool Contractor> will be in touch with you to finalize the maintenance agreement. We have been satisfied with their service, and I think the Board has made a wise choice to retain them.

If other questions regarding the care or operation of any mechanical features arise in the future, please contact me.

Sincerely,

[Builder]
cc: <Community homeowners>

Letters for Difficult Situations and Tough Customers

4

The letters that follow address regrettable situations—whether caused by circumstances beyond the builder's control, the builder's failure to perform as planned, or the undesirable behavior of the customers.

Regardless of the specific cause for your letter, state clearly that you are prepared to meet all contractual obligations. Remain calm and businesslike in your tone. Present the facts logically. List any options that may exist and come to an appropriate conclusion.

Your conclusion may request some action on the part of the customers. If so, include a reasonable deadline. One caution, avoid the false security of saying "If we do not hear from you we will assume . . ." Lack of action on the part of your customer does not guarantee closure of an issue.

For some letters you may want verification that the homeowners or other addressees received them. The U.S. Postal Service offers several options for obtaining written confirmation that your communication was received. Talk with a staff member at your local post office to determine which is appropriate for your needs.

Answering Angry Letters

Angry customers often resort to sarcasm, insult, and exaggeration in an effort to get a response. Service professionals must be adept at sifting through this emotional debris, identifying the issues, and responding.

❏ Copy the letter. File the original and work with the copy.

❏ Read the copy once. Make no notes, speak no expletives—just read.

❏ Put the letter off to one side until the next work day. The natural reaction, which is to become angry and defensive, needs time to dissipate.

❏ The next day, reread the letter, pen in hand. List each issue then prioritize the items.

❏ Review every item in the customer's file for background information.

❏ Talk with others who might have some input regarding the history of the situation or relationship.

❏ Determine whether a site visit or an inspection is needed and if so schedule it promptly.

❏ Once you have the facts, determine appropriate responses, issue by issue.

❏ Follow through on everything you agreed to do and document your response to each item for the file.

Extend Schedule ➜

The labor shortage facing the homebuilding industry is likely to be around for the foreseeable future. This fact, combined with overloaded building departments, material shortages (if you've missed the fun of rationed materials count yourself lucky), ever-present weather concerns, today's prolonged selection processes, and change orders all lead to unpredictable delivery dates. When you must move the target date, alert the buyers as soon as possible. The more time they have to react, the greater their chance of reducing inconvenience. Make a phone call and back it up with a letter. Figure 4.1 offers an example.

FIGURE 4.1 Extend Schedule

<Date>
<Home Buyer's Name>
<Address>
<City, State, and Zip Code>

Extend Schedule

Dear <Home Buyer>:

The excellent economic conditions we are all enjoying bring many benefits. They also come with a couple of challenges. One of these is a shortage of skilled labor for building new homes in a predictable time frame. Perhaps your profession faces similar labor shortages or you may have read articles in the papers and magazines describing this condition.

[Builder] prefers to work with companies we know and trust. Over the years, our trade contractors have become familiar with our quality standards and comfortable with our communication systems. We are reluctant to work with untested firms. As a result, we sometimes must wait for the work of those we know and trust.

Unfortunately, we cannot protect you from the result of this challenge we face. The construction schedule for your new home construction must be extended. The new target date is <date>, and this date may change again. We will provide a firm date a minimum of 30 days prior to your closing.

We regret any inconvenience this change causes you and hope that by providing you with this information now you can adjust your moving plans with a minimum of disruption.

If you have any questions, please contact me.

Sincerely,

[Builder]

Alternate Selection ➜

Manufacturers and suppliers have an uncanny knack for terminating production of the items home buyers have fallen in love with, selected, and perhaps paid extra for. When this situation occurs, prompt action is required to prevent delays in construction.

Begin by alerting the customer by phone and follow up with a letter such as the one shown in Figure 4.2. Express empathy for the inconvenience and set a clear time frame for the buyers to make a new choice.

FIGURE 4.2 Alternate Selection

<Date>
<Home Buyer's Name>
<Address>
<City, State, and Zip Code>

Alternate Selection

Dear <Home Buyer>:

<Supplier>, our tile supplier, has notified us that the tile you selected for your master bath is no longer available. They conducted a computer search of other suppliers which failed to locate the tile in sufficient quantities for your home. We sincerely regret this inconvenience.

At this time, please arrange to visit the Selection Center as soon as possible to choose an alternate tile. If you can select another tile by <date>, we can avoid any delay in the construction schedule.

The Selection Center is expecting your visit and will expedite getting the information through the system. The Center's phone number is—

<Selection Center phone number>

Although this situation is outside of our control, we understand that this is both a disappointment and an inconvenience for you. We appreciate your cooperation in this matter.

If you have any questions, please contact me.

Sincerely,

[Builder]
cc: Selection Center

Change in Design, Material, or Product ➔

Most purchase agreements say the builder has the right to "substitute equal or better materials or methods." However, genuine concern for home buyers' satisfaction means making a reasonable effort to alert buyers when you make significant changes. The question of whether a change is significant is a matter of judgement.

Often, if they are told in advance to expect a difference (Figure 4.3), buyers not only accept the change without complaints, but they also are impressed with your attention and forthright communication. Trust results.

FIGURE 4.3 Change in Design, Material, or Product

\<Date\>
\<Home Buyer's Name\>
\<Address\>
\<City, State, and Zip Code\>

Change in Product

Dear \<Home Buyer\>:

The specifications for your home describe the water heater as a \<brand, model, size\>.

The manufacturer ceased production of this model and it is now unavailable for your home. In its place we will install a \<brand, model, size\>. We reviewed features, operational costs, and manufacturers' warranties from over 10 different choices and selected this as the most comparable to the original.

We believe you will be satisfied with its performance.

If you have any questions, please contact me.

Sincerely,

[Builder]
cc: \<Superintendent\>
\<Sales Associate\>

Onsite Interference →

In the fourth edition of David Jaffe's book, *Contracts and Liability for Builders and Remodelers*, you will find this paragraph on page 28:

> The owners shall not in any manner interfere with work on the job nor with any subcontractor or workers. The owners will not communicate directly with the builder's workers, employees, agents, or subcontractors regarding the means, method, or manner in which they are to perform the work. If the owners delay the progress of the work, causing loss to the builder, the builder shall be entitled to reimbursement from the owner for such loss.[8]

While you may want to replace owners with purchasers or buyers, you should include this paragraph, reviewed by your attorney—or one similar to it developed by your attorney—in your purchase agreement. If jobsite interference occurs, begin with a casual in-person chat or a phone call about this issue. When a friendly conversation does not stop jobsite interference by a home buyer, you may decide to take a stronger stand. Take appropriate actions promptly because the longer the buyer's habit persists, the more difficult it is to stop. The sample letter in Figure 4.4 may assist you in composing such a letter.

FIGURE 4.4 Onsite Interference

\<Date\>
\<Home Buyer's Name\>
\<Address\>
\<City, State, and Zip Code\>

Onsite Interference

Dear \<Home Buyer\>:

Your interest in your new home is understandable. We appreciate that you want a high-quality product and value for your money. Our construction systems are designed to provide you with the quality and value we promised you in our contract documents and showed to you with our model homes.

To achieve this quality and value, [Builder] must direct and maintain control over the work. This issue is so important that the [Builder's] purchase agreement which you signed on \<date\> includes a clause which states:

> Purchasers shall not in any manner interfere with work on the job nor with any subcontractor or workers. Purchasers will not communicate directly with the builder's workers, employees, agents, or subcontractors regarding the means, method, or manner in which they are to perform the work. If Purchasers delay the progress of the work, causing loss to the builder, the builder shall be entitled to reimbursement from the owner for such loss.

On several occasions, conversations you have initiated with tradespeople and [Builder] employees have caused disruption of the work and confusion about methods and materials. We have asked that you communicate any questions you have only to your sales associate. [Builder] has a written system for tracking and responding to such concerns.

We ask that you respect this system and refrain from any further interference with work at the jobsite. [Builder] will pursue all avenues of recourse to recoup any losses caused by further interference.

We appreciate your cooperation in this matter. If you have any questions, please contact me.

Sincerely,

[Builder]
cc: \<Superintendent\>
\<Sales associate\>

Default Notification ➜

When provisions of a purchase agreement require that buyers perform specific tasks by specific deadlines and buyers fail to comply, they are in breach of contract. Builders must address these situations. Usually confronting a breach of contract begins in a low-key manner with a conversation. Too often, repeated conversations with the buyers produce promise on top of promise, yet the needed results do not follow. When builders allow these situations to linger beyond a reasonable time without taking definitive action, negative results increase.

The terms of your purchase agreement will describe the repercussions and your options when a default situation arises. Resolving the problem begins with putting the buyers on notice. You can provide this notice with a letter similar to the one in Figure 4.5. Curing the default within a specified time frame offers the buyers a chance to correct the violation.

If the buyers cure the default, the relationship continues. If they do not, contract termination is the next step, possibly followed by arbitration or legal action. Usually the sooner the builder acts in these situations, the less damage the company will suffer.

FIGURE 4.5 Default Notification

<Date>
<Home Buyer's Name>
<Address>
<City, State, and Zip Code>

Default Notification

Dear <Home Buyer>:

Regarding our purchase and sale agreement dated <date> and pertaining to the property described as <legal description and address>, you are hereby notified that you are in default of clause number <clause number> of the referenced purchase and sale agreement. This clause states—

<type in the clause buyer is in default of>

You have seven (7) days from the date of this notification to remedy this default.

If you fail to remedy this default within the time specified, [Builder] will retain your deposit as liquidated damages as described in the purchase agreement and the purchase agreement will be null and void.

If you have any questions, please contact me.

Sincerely,

[Builder]

Terminate Purchase Agreement ➜

If the buyer's default remains uncured, few options are available to the builder. Termination of a purchase agreement is unpleasant, but it is an improvement over some of the other possibilities—such as building a home and not getting paid.

By this point you would most likely be consulting with your company attorney. Explore every possible means to restore the agreement, but recognize when the time arrives to cut your losses. When all else fails, notify the buyers that you are terminating the purchase agreement (Figure 4.6).

FIGURE 4.6 Terminate Purchase Agreement

\<Date\>
\<Home Buyer's Name\>
\<Address\>
\<City, State, and Zip Code\>

Terminate Purchase Agreement

Dear \<Home Buyer\>:

Regarding our purchase agreement dated \<date\> and pertaining to the property described as \<legal description and address\>, you are hereby notified that [Builder] is exercising its rights under the terms of that agreement to terminate the agreement as described in clause number \<clause number\>.

This action is necessary because you have failed to cure the default of which we notified you on \<date\>. A copy of that notice is enclosed.

[Builder] will retain your deposit as liquidated damages as described in the purchase agreement, clause number \<clause number\> and the purchase agreement is now null and void.

If you have any questions, please contact me.

Sincerely,

[Builder]
Enclosure

Apology ➜

While customers for the most part understand that people are imperfect, that understanding does not justify a cavalier attitude when things go wrong. On occasion you may find yourself needing to express regret about an event.

Recovery skills begin with seeing clearly when you are at fault, accepting responsibility, and taking corrective action. Even when the circumstances are outside your control, empathizing with the home buyers' disappointment shows sensitivity and costs little. A dignified expression of regret can go a long way to make amends and show respect for your customers.

When an apology is in order, keep it businesslike and straight forward. Note that the sample letters (Figures 4.7 and 4.8) use the word *regret*, rather than the more personal, *sorry*. Outline the corrective measures you plan to take. Affirm your intention to fulfill your obligations as well as your commitment to customer satisfaction. These expressions will deflect many arguments and impress all but the most difficult customers.

FIGURE 4.7 Apology for Delayed Warranty Response

<Date>
<Homeowner's Name>
<Address>
<City, State, and Zip Code>

Apology for Delayed Warranty Response

Dear <Homeowner>:

Warranty work orders we issued for work in your home are behind schedule for completion.

We don't like this situation and we realize you don't either.

The cause is the volume of new home construction underway in our region. The trade contractors are struggling to keep up with demands for new homes and struggling to meet their warranty obligations to previously built homes.

We accept responsibility for addressing this problem. However, in spite of our efforts, we cannot completely protect you from the effects.

We want to assure you that we monitor warranty work orders for timely completion and are aware that your home needs work. We will continue to track your work order and communicate with trade contractors and you to see that all work ordered is completed.

Your patience is appreciated, and if you have any questions, please contact me.

Sincerely,

[Builder]

FIGURE 4.8 Apology for Damage to Personal Items

<Date>
<Homeowner's Name>
<Address>
<City, State, and Zip Code>

Apology for Damage to Personal Items

Dear <Homeowner>:

Thank you for your phone call regarding the <damage> that occurred in your home on <date>.

We contacted the trade contractor involved, and the company will be compensating you for your loss. Our warranty office will follow up with you on the details of this damage.

[Builder] regrets you had this experience. As a result we are reviewing our policies and communication systems in an effort to prevent a recurrence.

If you have any questions, please contact me.

Sincerely,

[Builder]
cc: <Trade contractor>

Material Defect ➜

In spite of a builder's best efforts, from time to time defective materials or methods may be used in several homes before any problem appears. Powered by rumors, anger, and fear, news of this type travels through a community at an alarming rate. Hiding or appearing to sidestep responsibility can lead to worse problems than facing the situation squarely. Some people will argue that the builder should remain silent and respond only when and if homeowners, the news media, or others contact the builder. They suggest that calling attention to the problem obligates the company to more repairs and acknowledges legal responsibility. Each situation is different. When you find yourself in a "damned if you do, damned if you don't" position, consider whether you prefer to be found damned on the high road or cowering under your desk.

Often a head-on approach by the builder can allay homeowners' fears and capture the respect (and cooperation) of the customers affected. The letter that follows (Figure 4.9 with enclosure Figure 4.10) shows one way to address such a situation. Effective follow-through supported with detailed documentation is essential for this approach to be successful.

Sources of Material Defects:

- Flaws in product design—all of the product can show defects.
- One batch of product turns out to be defective.
- Installation errors.
- Improper maintenance by the homeowner.

Techniques for Minimizing Such Catastrophes:

- Select materials with long-term performance in mind.
- Avoid basing decisions solely on cost.
- Review manufacturers' installation instructions in detail and follow them.
- Consider having a manufacturer's rep inspect your work and sign off on your installation.
- Maintain accurate and complete files so you can determine what materials you used where.
- Include appropriate maintenance information in your homeowner manual.

For more information on managing this and other service challenges, see *Customer Relations Handbook for Builders.*[9]

FIGURE 4.9 Material Defect

<Date>
<Homeowner's Name>
<Address>
<City, State, and Zip Code>

Homeowner Bulletin

Dear <Homeowner>

Several [Builder] homeowners have contacted us regarding concerns over windows, including water leaks and what may be excessive air infiltration.

As a result, we are conducting an investigation to determine whether the problems experienced are caused by an error in installation or a faulty product.

If the installation is the cause, [Builder] will correct this. If the product is faulty, we will work with the supplier and manufacturer to correct the concerns reported. We have initiated a dialog with the supplier and the manufacturer about this matter.

In a situation of this type, good data is essential. We need a complete list of which homes and which windows may be involved. You can assist in this effort by providing us with information about your home.

Please use the Window Survey form enclosed to alert us to any concerns you have about your windows. Normally, some air and even dust may infiltrate windows, especially on high-wind days and while the area around your home is not yet landscaped. However, excessive air or any water is unacceptable.

If you indicate any concerns on the enclosed form, we will contact you for an inspection and will keep you informed regarding our findings and actions. You can expect an update on the response from the supplier and manufacturer within the next several weeks.

Your assistance with this investigation is appreciated.

Sincerely,

[Builder]
Enclosure

FIGURE 4.10 Window Survey Form

Window Survey

Date_____

Name_____

Address_____

Phone_____

❏ The windows in my home are performing satisfactorily.

❏ I have concerns about windows in the following rooms and would like an inspection.

_____

_____

_____

_____

_____

_____

_____

_____

**Please note that condensation is caused by humidity
within the home and is not considered a leak.**

_____   _____
Homeowner   Date

Denied Warranty Claims →

The seven letters that follow (Figures 4.11 through 4.17) address various situations leading to the builder denying warranty action. These examples include warranty claims for—

- maintenance items (Figure 4.11)

- homeowners' association maintenance items in a multifamily community (Figure 4.12)

- an item added to the home by the homeowner, not part of the home as purchased from the builder (Figure 4.13)

- homeowner alterations to grading that resulted in a drainage problem (Figure 4.14)

- an item not within the scope of the warranty (Figure 4.15)

- homeowner damage to the home (Figure 4.16)

- a difference in standards between the builder's product and the homeowner's expectations (Figure 4.17)

In each of these situations, the builder is able to deny the claim because complete information was provided to the buyer up front, the builder had excellent documentation for back up, and the commitment made by the builder in the initial agreement was substantially fulfilled. In other words, the builder is operating from a position of strength.

FIGURE 4.11 Homeowner's Maintenance Item

<Date>
<Homeowner's Name>
<Address>
<City, State, and Zip Code>

Homeowner's Maintenance Item

Dear <Homeowner>:

Your warranty service request, dated <date>, listed seven items which <warranty representative> inspected on <date>. We issued the enclosed work orders on <date> as a result of that inspection. Two items, the concrete cracks you noted in item 4 and drywall cracks you noted in number 7, remain to be addressed.

According to the terms of our agreement with you, concrete cracks that exceed 3/16 inch in width or vertical displacement qualify for warranty action (filling or patching). The crack in your garage floor is located in the control joint and is less than 1/8 inch. The crack in your patio is hairline. Neither crack has measurable displacement. Because these cracks are within the agreed upon standards, no action is required. You can review this information on page <page number> of your *[Builder] Homeowner Manual*. Attention to these cracks is a home maintenance issue, and therefore you are responsible for repairing them.

The drywall damage (two hairline cracks in the family room, a corner bead in the nook, and three nail pops in the sunroom) are typical of those we commonly see as new homes settle. As a courtesy, we will have the painter caulk and touch up the paint. The new paint will be visible; an exact match is unlikely. You can review this information on page <page number> of your *Homeowner Manual*.

Your copy of the work order to the painter, <name of painter>, is enclosed.

If you have any questions, please contact me.

Sincerely,

[Builder]
Enclosure

FIGURE 4.12 Maintenance Items for the Homeowners' Association

<Date>
<Homeowner's Name>
<Address>
<City, State, and Zip Code>

Homeowners' Association Maintenance Items

Dear <Homeowner>:

Your warranty service request, dated <date>, and listing problems with exterior lights and paint for shutters on your townhome arrived today.

The maintenance service provided by the <Community> Homeowners' Association includes care of these items. The Association designates a portion of the dues you pay each month for this type of exterior maintenance, and they have a regular schedule for this and other maintenance service.

I have forwarded your request to the association's managing agent, <name of managing agent>, with a copy of this letter.

In addition, I suggest you follow up with the managing agent by calling <phone number of managing agent>.

If you have any questions, please contact me.

Sincerely,

[Builder]
cc: <Managing agent>

FIGURE 4.13 Item Added to House by Purchaser

\<Date>
\<Homeowner's Name>
\<Address>
\<City, State, and Zip Code>

Item Added to House by Homeowner

Dear \<Homeowner>:

This letter confirms our conversation of this morning.

Your warranty service request, dated \<date>, regarding \<item> arrived today. The documents in your file omit any mention of \<item>. Our limited warranty covers the home as purchased from [Builder] and specifically excludes items you add to the home after purchasing it from us.

If our information is in error, please let us know. Otherwise, I recommend you contact the retailer from whom you purchased \<item> for assistance.

If you have any questions, please contact me.

Sincerely,

[Builder]

FIGURE 4.14 Grading Altered

<Date>
<Homeowner's Name>
<Address>
<City, State, and Zip Code>

Grading Altered

Dear <Homeowner>:

In response to your report of drainage concerns in your side yard, we reviewed the grading certificate for your property and had the grades rechecked by our surveyors. Copies of both readings are enclosed.

This review shows that the drainage swale on the east side of your home has been changed significantly. Often the cause of this type of change is that the soil from holes dug for shrubs or trees is spread over adjacent areas. This change may be what occurred in your yard.

Two choices are available to you to restore good drainage. One is to recreate the original swale. The second is to install a French drain. Please refer to your *[Builder] Homeowner Manual* for detailed information.

Either action would be your responsibility. However, you may have recourse with the landscaping company that did this work.

Remember, your warranty specifically excludes damage resulting from changes in grading.

Sincerely,

[Builder]
Enclosures

FIGURE 4.15 Outside the Scope of Warranty

<Date>
<Homeowner's Name>
<Address>
<City, State, and Zip Code>

Outside the Scope of Warranty

Dear <Homeowner>:

This letter is to confirm the conclusion of our meeting on <date>, regarding your warranty service request dated, <date>, asking that [Builder] remove the snakes from the open space that runs along the back edge of your lot.

As we discussed, the [Builder's] limited warranty covers only the home you purchased from us and does not extend to the open space behind your property.

Further, the limited warranty specifically excludes insect and animal activity. The state wildlife division at <phone>, will be mailing information to you regarding snakes and snake safety.

I hope this information will be helpful. If you have any questions, please contact me.

Sincerely,

[Builder]

FIGURE 4.16 Damage Caused by Homeowner

<Date>
<Homeowner's Name>
<Address>
<City, State, and Zip Code>

Damage Caused by Homeowner

Dear <Homeowner>:

This letter is to confirm our conversation regarding your warranty service request dated <date>.

The items listed—a carpet stain in the family room and a 1-inch long cut in the vinyl in the laundry room—are examples of the cosmetic damage referred to on your orientation form. One of the purposes of the orientation is to confirm the home is in acceptable condition. Your orientation forms show your agreement that the home was in acceptable condition.

After the orientation, this type of damage is specifically excluded from warranty coverage. These items fall into that category. Therefore, [Builder] can assist you with information, but repairs are your responsibility.

The flooring contractor—<name, phone>—who did the original work on your home can assist you with both of these items. The contractor may be able to clean the spot from the carpet or, if that proves unsuccessful, they can patch it.

A patch of the laundry room vinyl is possible, or you can have the entire floor covering replaced.

Payment for attention to either item will be your responsibility.

If you have any questions, please contact me.

Sincerely,

[Builder]
cc: <Flooring contractor>

FIGURE 4.17 Difference in Standards

<Date>
<Homeowner's Name>
<Address>
<City, State, and Zip Code>

Difference in Standards

Dear <Homeowner>:

In response to your warranty service request, dated <date>, we inspected the items you listed on <date>. We have issued work orders on four items. Copies of those work orders are enclosed.

As we discussed during the inspection of your list, the finish on the hardwood floor in the kitchen and nook areas is showing the normal effects of use and requires no warranty attention. Please refer to your *[Builder] Homeowner Manual* and to the manufacturer's brochure you received at your orientation for complete details on caring for this flooring.

If you have any questions, please contact me.

Sincerely,

[Builder]
Enclosures

Repetitious Warranty Requests ➔

In spite of a clear description of your warranty procedures, some buyers will submit list after list. This practice impacts the efficiency of the warranty staff and trade contractors. Equally or even more serious, overlapping lists create confusion, and they duplicate efforts when items already listed on work orders are listed again. The technician receiving the second work order has no way of knowing whether the item has already been corrected or failed a second time.

Under these circumstances, the goals of customer satisfaction and operational efficiency come into conflict. The builder faces a choice between dealing with the confusion or asking the homeowners to exercise restraint until normal checkpoints occur. Further complicating this issue is the reality that most warranty documents state that if homeowners notice an item, fail to report it, and additional damage results, the builder can deny the claim.

The best approach seems to be to discuss this calmly with the homeowners and ask permission to hold nonemergency items until a preset time for warranty attention. Figure 4.18 offers a written follow-up to the in-person conversation or phone call. However, remember that homeowners have no obligation to limit their warranty expectations to the one or two dates selected by their builders. If the homeowners persist, be a good sport and process the items cheerfully.

FIGURE 4.18 Repetitious Warranty Requests

<Date>
<Homeowner's Name>
<Address>
<City, State, and Zip Code>

Confirm Repairs and Standard Checkpoints

Dear <Homeowner>:

This letter confirms our conversation of this afternoon. As we discussed, in response to your warranty service requests dated <date>, <date>, <date>, and <date>, I have issued work orders to the appropriate trade contractors.

Your next standard warranty contact will be near the end of your materials and workmanship warranty, during <month>. [Builder] created this system of standard contacts to provide efficient service to all of our homeowners, and we appreciate your cooperation with the standard system.

Now that I explained the reasons for our system, I hope that you will be comfortable working within the standard checkpoints.

Certainly, if an emergency occurs you should call us or, outside our business hours, the appropriate trade contractor. If a particular item is causing you great inconvenience, submit a warranty service request. Otherwise our next contact with you will be in <month>.

If you have any questions, please contact me.

Sincerely,

[Builder]

Demand that You Move Furniture ➜

An earlier letter (Figure 4.8) apologized to homeowners for damage to a personal item that occurred during warranty work. Prevention is much better. The simplest approach is to ask homeowners to remove vulnerable personal items from the work area when workers are in the home.

However, homeowners often view moving large pieces of furniture as the builder's responsibility. Their attitude is—"After all, you built the house wrong." The letter that follows (Figure 4.19) addresses a situation requiring work on hardwood floors damaged during construction. The homeowners' $14,000 entertainment system (whenever homeowners mention the cost of their furnishings, take heed) needed to be moved out of the family room for this work to be done. The homeowners insisted that builder personnel move the entertainment system.

Anticipating repercussions, the builder decided against moving this equipment and a disagreement followed. Resolution came when the builder sent this letter and waited for a reply.

The builder decided that the best choice was to offer to pay the cost of the repair and thereby risk that the corrective work would not be performed (leaving a defective home for all to see). The builder was willing to accept that risk compared to the risk of moving the entertainment center and paying for that as well as the floor work.

Warranty Clause: Builder's Obligation

Be certain your limited warranty provides you with all the options the law allows for resolving warranty items. This clause provides three choices.

If a covered defect occurs during the one-year warranty period, the Company agrees to repair, replace, or pay the Owner the reasonable cost of repairing or replacing the defective item. The Company's total liability under this warranty is limited to the purchase price of the home as stated above. The choice among repair, replacement, or payment is the Company's. Any steps taken by the Company to correct defects shall not act to extend the terms of this warranty. All repairs done by the Company shall be at no charge to the Owner and shall be performed within a reasonable length of time.[10]

FIGURE 4.19 Demand that Builder Move Furniture

\<Date\>
\<Homeowner's Name\>
\<Address\>
\<City, State, and Zip Code\>

Demand that Builder Move Furniture

Dear \<Homeowner\>:

Work order number \<work order number\> was issued on \<date\> for warranty work needed for the hardwood floors in your home.

In all work that we perform for our homeowners, we are concerned about their personal belongings and want them to be protected. The work needed on your hardwood floors is extensive, and therefore your safest course is to remove all furnishings from the affected area (kitchen, nook, entry hall, and family room).

To perform this work without risk to your personal belongings, the entertainment system in the family room will also need to be removed from the work area. We are unable to move the entertainment center, and therefore we ask that you move it prior to the work being performed.

If you prefer not to move these items, we will issue a check to you for the cost of the work, \<\$_____\>.

Please initial your choice below, sign, and return this letter to schedule an appointment or to receive a check. (We need to provide the flooring contractor with a minimum of 7 days notice.) If you have any questions, please call me.

Sincerely,

[Builder]

❏ Please contact me to schedule the work on the hardwood floors. We will remove the entertainment center and all other personal belongings from the work area prior to the work appointment.

❏ We hereby accept the payment quoted above in lieu of corrective work on the hardwood floors in our home. We understand that acceptance of payment in this matter constitutes a complete release of [Builder] for this warranty claim.

_____   _____
Homeowner   Date

Wait to Wallpaper →

After working to cure a persistent and serious roof leak, a builder received as a faxed memo the text shown below and was in a quandary as to how to respond. Without attempting to analyze the motives or logic of the homeowner, the builder wanted to respond in a way that was positive but that still protected the company from what could clearly be a potentially expensive future claim. The response follows in Figure 4.20.

No leaks for approximately 2 months now!!! While the "rain" tests have not been what they would be in the spring, I think we can proceed and repair the inside water damage, including the bay window, the foyer, and the master bedroom.

You advised that you would be in touch to schedule repair work. I would like to get this completed as soon as possible as I would like to proceed with wallpapering my home!

I am concerned that the spring will bring heavy rains and leaks will resurface. *I'd like to get your intentions in writing as to your repair plan should this happen.*

I'm hopeful that this will be the last time we need to communicate on this issue. I wish you well in your business and am looking forward to finally being able to enjoy my home.

Thanks for your prompt attention to this memo.

Roof Leaks

To manage customer expectations, provide a candid explanation and commitment to the homeowner, including the following points.

- Repairs cannot be made while the roof is wet because it is slippery and dangerous.
- The repair order will be given top priority on the next dry day.
- We will not know whether the repair has been successful until Mother Nature tests the repair.

We will contact you after the next several rains to check on the status of the repair.

FIGURE 4.20 Wait to Wallpaper

\<Date\>
\<Homeowner's Name\>
\<Address\>
\<City, State, and Zip Code\>

Wait to Wallpaper

Dear \<Homeowner\>:

Thank you for your update, dated \<date\>, regarding the leak repair. I am delighted to hear that the work we have done has been successful and we all share your hope that a permanent resolution has been achieved.

Builders and homeowners alike find weather-related leaks—involving basements, windows, roofs, and so on—to be extremely frustrating. The reason of course is that builders perform repairs and then all parties wait for Mother Nature to test the work.

Based on your reporting that no further problems have occurred during the last 2 months, we will proceed with the drywall repairs. However, I caution you against any custom decorating until after the spring weather has provided you and [Builder] with a more thorough testing.

While I understand that you are anxious to personalize your home, please be aware that should any further problems occur with this issue, our warranty coverage will provide repairs to the structure. Our repair would also include restoring the home to the same condition and finish as at delivery. However, our warranty specifically excludes repairs to decorating materials, including wallpaper or custom paint colors, that you install.

We intend, as we always have, to stand behind our product and to fulfill all warranty obligations. Consequential and secondary damages are excluded from this coverage, however. Therefore installation of wallpaper or custom paint colors would be at your risk.

If you experience any further leakage, please contact us immediately, and we will schedule an inspection. Thank you for your cooperation and good wishes. We sincerely wish you every happiness in your [Builder] home.

Sincerely,

[Builder]

Disagreement with Neighbor ➜

When they imagine living in their new homes, few home buyers include disagreements with their future neighbors. However, such a situation can occur and often a homeowner's first action is to take the issue to the builder without communicating with the offending neighbor.

Providing positive suggestions like those listed in the letter to the complaining homeowner (Figure 4.21) can help improve communications. When these complaints are based on drainage concerns, the builder's best interest involves getting the matter effectively resolved. Water draining from a neighbor's yard can impact the foundation on an adjoining lot. Such situations are better avoided. Solid information about landscaping responsibilities backed by reasonable homeowners' association rules can minimize such situations.

FIGURE 4.21 Disagreement with Neighbor

<Date>
<Homeowner's Name>
<Address>
<City, State, and Zip Code>

Disagreement with Neighbor

Dear <Homeowner>:

Your letter of <date> regarding your concern about your neighbor's landscaping arrived today.

[Builder] provides the same landscaping information to all home buyers. Beyond advising home buyers about the proper installation and maintenance of their yards, [Builder] has no authority to enforce the recommendations we provide.

We suggest you approach the neighbor with your concerns. Often a homeowner does not consider the impact of grading changes on adjacent yards.

[Builder] can provide documentation regarding the overall drainage plan for the community. Finally, your Homeowners' Association has strict rules regarding landscaping, and plans must be approved by the Design Review Committee. To contact them, call <chairperson> at <phone number>. <He or She> can provide you with specific details and current regulations.

If you have any questions, please contact me.

Sincerely,

[Builder]

Demand for Cash ➜

Home buyers may experience "selective vision"—seeing what they want to see—during the home shopping process. Later they may be disappointed with details they failed to notice. They may express displeasure and ask or demand a refund on the offending item. In conversations about such matters builders frequently hear, "In a home of this price. . . ."

Less frequently (fortunately) but still a reality (unfortunately) is the dishonest customer who zeros in on an item, usually cosmetic, and feigns dissatisfaction for the sole purpose of financial gain.[11]

When builders operate from a position of strength—communicate forthrightly throughout the process, deliver on promises, and document every detail—they are better able to deflect such claims. The letter in Figure 4.22 provides sample wording for a response. Notice the optional offer to replace the item in question. This option may be feasible in some cases, and it offers a potential compromise. A fair-minded customer, one with a problem-solving mind set, is likely to accept this solution.

FIGURE 4.22 Demand for Cash

<Date>
<Homeowner's Name>
<Address>
<City, State, and Zip Code>

Demand for Cash

Dear <Homeowner>:

In response to your phone call on <date> regarding your disappointment with <item>, I reviewed the documents in your file as I promised.

Although [Builder] offers several upgrade options for <item>, your selection form lists the standard <item>, and it was installed in your home.

If <item> fails to meet the warranty guidelines described on page <page number> of your *[Builder] Homeowner Manual*, we will provide appropriate repairs. Our service policies exclude reimbursing you for the cost of this item based on your dissatisfaction with it. It is correct according to the order for your home and is functioning as designed.

[Optional] If you are willing to pay for installation, <cost>, and the cost difference between your original selection and your choice of one of the available upgrades, we can arrange for replacement.

If you wish to proceed with this alternative, please contact <selection coordinator> no later than <date> and arrange an appointment to complete the necessary paper work and pay the related costs. We will then schedule the work.

If you have any questions, please contact me.

Sincerely,

[Builder]
cc: <Selection coordinator>

Consequential Damages ➜

With few exceptions (where prohibited by law), builder warranties exclude compensation to homeowners for consequential or secondary damages. For instance, if a roof leak damaged drywall and a couch, the builder repairs the roof and the drywall. The couch damage is consequential or secondary, and it becomes a concern for the homeowner and possibly the homeowner's insurance company.

> The value of confirming the condition of the work area—in writing if he or she finds any damage—before and after work is an excellent topic to cover with in-house and trade contractors' service personnel.

At least that is the theory. In practice, builders often make exceptions to this stated policy. Each case must be considered on an individual basis. Figure 4.23 denies reimbursement for a homeowner's hotel bill while Figure 4.24 compensates a homeowner for damage that allegedly occurred to an area rug during repair work. A distinction to consider is the difference between secondary damage that occurs as a result of a warranted failure (such as a roof leak) and damage that occurs during repair activity performed by someone the builder sent to the home. A homeowner typically has insurance that may cover consequential damages, but the homeowner's insurance is unlikely to cover damage done by a worker sent to the home.

FIGURE 4.23 Reimbursement for Consequential Damage Denied

<Date>
<Homeowner's Name>
<Address>
<City, State, and Zip Code>

Reimbursement for Consequential Damage Denied

Dear <Homeowner>:

Your letter dated, <date>, and receipts for two nights in a hotel arrived today.

On rare occasions [Builder] needs to ask a family to vacate their home while we perform repairs. In such cases we arrange hotel accommodations at a location where we have a corporate account, and we provide the family with a per diem for meals and incidentals.

In reviewing your situation, I found no information that anyone from [Builder] authorized this particular hotel stay. The repairs to your <repair item> did not require that the family vacate the home.

Therefore these expenses remain your responsibility.

If you have any questions, please contact me.

Sincerely,

[Builder]

FIGURE 4.24 Reimbursing Homeowner for Consequential Damage

<Date>
<Homeowner's Name>
<Address>
<City, State, and Zip Code>

Reimbursing Homeowner for Consequential Damage

Dear <Homeowner>:

Your fax of <date> regarding damage to the area rug in your family room arrived yesterday.

[Builder] has always found <trade contractor>, who performed the repair to the crown molding in your family room, to be reputable and honest. They have shown integrity and a commitment to quality many times over the years we have worked together.

I also believe your description of events and agree with your observation that they may have been unaware of having caused this damage. A conversation with them confirmed they do not believe they damaged the area rug.

Your letter sets the value of this rug at $400. While our service policies preclude a cash payment under these circumstances, in appreciation of your loss, we have enclosed a gift certificate in the amount of $400 for Rugs-R-Us. <Rugs-R-Us contact and contact's phone number> is expecting to hear from you and will assist you in selecting a replacement.

We regret any inconvenience this has caused you. If you have any questions, please contact me.

Sincerely,

[Builder]
Enclosure
cc: <Trade contractor>

Structural Warranty Claim →

Few homeowners experience structural problems. This situation is fortunate for home builders because structural repairs are costly, time-consuming, and emotionally trying for everyone. Avoiding such problems is desirable. However, the builder's job does not end with building a lasting and stable structure. The relationship with the buyer must be equally lasting and stable.

The letter that follows (Figure 4.25) responds to a letter from a homeowner whose home experienced a slight structural movement. He explained that a job transfer to another state was possible and asked what action the builder would take regarding the home if the transfer became a reality.

The homeowner further characterized the damage to the home as far more serious than it actually was. Worried about the financial repercussions of selling a home that was structurally unstable, the homeowner implied he was considering legal action.

The letter in return walks some fine lines. It aims to (a) reassure the homeowner without making promises the builder is not sure can be kept and (b) put the damage to the home in perspective without appearing unsympathetic. Another goal was to avoid challenging the homeowner's threat of legal action or appearing to be intimidated by it. The letter also appropriately tables the job transfer issue until more information is available.

Ultimately, the home was successfully repaired, the job transfer came through, and the homeowner sold the home with full disclosure at market price. Everyone lived happily ever after except those concerned about the warranty budget. (Repairs totaled nearly $14,000.)

FIGURE 4.25 Structural Warranty Claim

<Date>
<Homeowner's Name>
<Address>
<City, State, and Zip Code>

Structural Warranty Claim

Dear <Homeowner>:

In response to your letter, dated <date>, I hope the following information will answer the questions and concerns you expressed and help you to reassess your position.

[Builder] is as dismayed by these events as you and your family are. Some of the best available soil analysis, engineering talent, technical knowledge, and construction skills were combined to build your home. You have added your own financial and emotional investment. In this case, our soils refuse to respect even this impressive collection of efforts and commitments.

If any builder could construct a home with an absolute assurance that no problems would ever occur, we would need no warranties. A certain percentage of homes in our state, their builders and owners, are victimized by our soils. We all work with the results. I would be lax in stating our position in this matter if I did not point out that to date none of the engineer's inspections have identified any construction or engineering defect that could be held accountable for the movement we have observed. Your installation of landscaping and maintenance of backfill areas has been equally commendable.

[Builder]'s commitment to you remains unchanged. We intend to fulfill all contractual and warranty obligations. Although I cannot answer the question of what is a reasonable duration for resolution of this challenge, I believe we are proceeding as rapidly as circumstances permit. As difficult as they are to endure, the time periods to monitor the effects of corrective actions are as important as the actions themselves.

You referred to foundation cracks as "fundamental" and commented that these cannot be repaired. Fortunately, this assumption is incorrect. If a foundation crack exceeds 1/8 inch, an epoxy can be used to fill it. This forms a bond that is stronger than the original concrete. The epoxy material is darker in color and will be visible. More extreme repairs are available, but I do not expect the engineers will require any such measures for your home.

Similarly, bows in walls and ceilings can be repaired. Our trades do excellent cosmetic work on repairs, and when the time comes, they will restore your home to within the [Builder] standards you found appealing when you purchased your home.

Regarding the possibility of a job transfer, we would discuss this with you when and if it occurs. I'm certain you can appreciate that we would need to take a great many variables—in particular the condition of the home at the time of such a transfer—into account. We cannot state our position on this issue at this time because too many questions remain unanswered.

As you requested, I will outline our intention for the next 60 to 90 days.

We have recently checked and cleared the void under the crawl space of your foundation. We found it to be in good to excellent condition. Our present schedule calls for re-establishing more heavily loaded caissons in this area during the month of <month>.

If no further movement occurs, cosmetic repairs can follow in late <month>. We will make a complete and detailed list for this work and will paint all repairs. The engineer will make several inspections during this time period. As soon as the engineer believes we have stopped the movement, we will proceed with cosmetic repairs.

Installation of a drain line along the west and north sides of your property is also scheduled to occur in <month>.

I understand your need to reassess your position in this matter. If you have any further questions, please contact me.

Sincerely,

[Builder]

Consumer Protection Entity ➔

In a behavior called *system skipping*, homeowners report warranty items to the Better Business Bureau, a licensing board, or another consumer protection entity without ever having reported them to the builder. Embarrassed by what feels like a reprimand from the consumer protection entity, the builder's staff may resent the situation—and the homeowners. This reaction is unproductive; the consumer protection entity is just doing its job. These professionals are well aware of today's consumers' attitudes and will give you a chance to share your side of the situation. Energy is better put into inspecting the items and providing needed repairs.

When a plan of action is in place, the builder can take the healing step of informing the consumer protection entity about the repairs the builder is providing (Figure 4.26). A secondary follow-up that often works well is a call to the homeowners to review normal reporting procedures and to assure the homeowners that by following these procedures, the builder's response can be provided faster. After all, the processing time at the consumer protection entity is eliminated.

The builder might also want to remind the home buyer that the warranty documents state that if homeowners notice an item, fail to report it to the builder, and additional damage results, the builder can deny the claim. The contract also requires the homeowners to give such notice and provide the builder an opportunity to correct it.

Customers who behave in this manner often have had serious problems with previous builders, or they may approach every customer service situation as if it were a battle. Gaining their trust takes extra work, but once they are convinced of your integrity, their praise is often enthusiastic because they have such negatives for comparison.

FIGURE 4.26 Consumer Protection Entity Notice

<Date>
<Consumer Protection Entity>
<Address>
<City, State, and Zip Code>

Consumer Protection Notice

Dear <Name of contact person>:

Your notice number <identifying case number> regarding <homeowner> arrived on <date>, and we contacted <homeowner> on the same day to schedule an inspection appointment.

The inspection occurred <date>. As a result, [Builder] has issued three work orders to appropriate trade contractors and one to an in-house service technician (copies enclosed). All work listed should be complete by <date>.

We found one item listed by the homeowners to be a normal home maintenance item, service for which is excluded from our warranty. We have informed the homeowners in writing of this fact.

A review of our file for this home established that the homeowners had not previously reported any of these items to us for attention. Therefore we have reviewed normal reporting procedures with the homeowners in hopes of expediting any further warranty repairs needed in their home.

We appreciate your attention to this matter. If you have any questions, please contact me.

Sincerely,

[Builder]
Enclosures

Warranty Void ➔

When homeowners fail to maintain their property, serious damage can occur. When this situation happens, the same homeowners often expect the builder to provide repairs. Again the builder is better off being the first to mention a subject. Figure 4.27 offers sample wording to put homeowners on notice that subsequent damage caused by their action (or inaction) will not be repaired by the builder. The optional paragraph can be used when hope exists that the homeowners will take prompt corrective action; the threat of a voided warranty often motivates responsible homeowners.

FIGURE 4.27 Warranty Void

<Date>
<Homeowner's Name>
<Address>
<City, State, and Zip Code>

Warranty Void

Dear <Homeowner>:

On <date>, I made a routine visit to <Community>, and I noticed the landscaping work you have had done in your front yard.

While the result is beautiful, the new berm at the front (northeast) corner of your home prevents water from draining away from the foundation of your home. Sprinkler heads between the berm and the house, which were operating when I was there, add extra water to this area and make this concern even more serious.

These conditions can cause structural damage to your home's foundation. Please review the landscaping guidelines and the [Builder] limited warranty. This information was part of the purchase agreement you signed to have us build your new home. I have enclosed copies of both with this letter for your convenience.

Because actions you have taken can cause damage to your home, the structural warranty coverage provided by [Builder] might be void. I urge you to contact your landscapers immediately and arrange corrections that will prevent structural damage.

If you have any questions, please contact me.

Sincerely,

[Builder]
Enclosures

Expired Warranty →

Builders sometimes believe that when the clock strikes midnight on the last day of homeowners' material and workmanship warranty, the company's obligation ends. Perhaps just as often, homeowners believe their builder will continue to service their home after the warranty has expired. Both assumptions can be erroneous.

Many conditions can result in a builder correcting items after the warranty expiration date. The builder should evaluate each situation individually. This evaluation includes listening to the homeowners' reasoning, investigating claims objectively, and arriving at fair decisions. When your decision is that the items are home maintenance responsibilities, the homeowners must be told promptly and courteously. Figure 4.28 shows such a response.

Note that this letter documents an earlier conversation that took place during a company inspection. (Accurate warranty decisions are seldom made from behind a desk. You need to get out to see the people and their homes.) When dealing with such situations, avoid negatives such as "that's not covered by warranty" and instead focus on what is true: this repair is a home maintenance item. Offer information you have that might assist the homeowners in taking care of the item. This information might include sending a copy of the appropriate pages from your homeowner manual or referring the homeowners to the manual. As always, say you are available to answer further questions.

Out of Warranty

Make sure your customers and your employees understand the circumstances under which your obligation continues even if the warranty has expired, including:

- a reasonable grace period
- code violation
- contract item
- previously reported item
- recurring item
- manufacturer-covered item

Others may occur. Give your homeowners the courtesy of a fair and thorough review.

FIGURE 4.28 Expired Warranty

<Date>
<Homeowner's Name>
<Address>
<City, State, and Zip Code>

Expired Warranty

Dear <Homeowner>:

This letter confirms our conversation of Tuesday, <month, date, year>, regarding your warranty service request, dated <date>.

The materials and workmanship coverage provided by [Builder's] limited warranty expired on <date>. Our inspection on <day, date> confirms that the items you listed are normal home maintenance tasks.

For specific information on how to proceed, please refer to the "Caring for Your Home" section of the *[Builder] Homeowner Manual*. As we discussed, the components of your home are listed alphabetically, and the entries include guidelines on maintenance.

If, after reviewing the information in the manual, you have additional questions, please contact me. I will be happy to discuss these maintenance tasks with you.

Sincerely,

[Builder]

Referral to Warranty Insurance ➜

If an insurance-backed warranty is part of the coverage you provide homeowners, from time to time you may need to refer homeowners to the standards and provisions that policy contains as the letter in Figure 4.29 does. This letter can be an effective approach when homeowners are dissatisfied with normal repair methods or believe the quality of work they received was unacceptable. Rather than endure escalating arguments and repeated inspections, sometimes a builder will get closure more quickly and be treated more objectively by a third party from the insurance company.

FIGURE 4.29 Referral to Warranty Insurance

<Date>
<Homeowner's Name>
<Address>
<City, State, and Zip Code>

Referral to Warranty Insurance

Dear <Homeowner>:

As part of your new home purchase, [Builder] provided an insurance-backed warranty policy. You received information about this warranty as part of your purchase agreement, again at the closing on your home purchase, and in the mail from <insurer> shortly after the closing.

That policy includes standards addressing <component or repair in dispute>. A copy of the standards booklet for this coverage is enclosed for your convenience.

While we regret you are dissatisfied with the repair we provided, we believe we have fulfilled the terms of our agreement with you.

If after reviewing the terms of these agreements, you still believe our attention to <item> fails to meet the standards listed, you may want to contact <insurer> to file a claim. In addition to specifying standards and repairs, <warranty insurer> provides for arbitration in the event of a dispute.

If you have any questions, please contact me.

Sincerely,

[Builder]

Referral to Attorney ➜

Some homeowners may believe they have legitimate claims that have gone unanswered; others may threaten you based on real or imagined issues in order to gain a financial settlement. Either way, your best defense is to seek legal counsel earlier rather than later. When homeowners have their attorney write to you, the most appropriate action is usually to have your attorney respond. Unless you have formal legal training, your conversation or correspondence with the homeowners' attorney can easily make a bad situation worse.

Write a rough draft containing the main points you believe need to be covered in the response and ask your attorney to compose and send the final letter. If your documents include a provision for alternative dispute resolution (ADR), such as arbitration or mediation, and depending on the circumstances, your attorney's response may point this out.

As a courtesy and to forestall any accusation that you ignored the homeowners' attorney, advise the homeowners that you have turned the matter over to your attorney. Your letter should avoid speculation, character analysis, or an evaluation of the claim in dispute. Figure 4.30 shows a matter-of-fact way to accomplish this goal.

FIGURE 4.30 Referral to Attorney

\<Date\>
\<Homeowner's Name\>
\<Address\>
\<City, State, and Zip Code\>

Referral to Attorney

Dear \<Homeowner\>:

The letter, dated \<date\>, from your attorney, \<name\>, arrived today.

We have forwarded this letter and copies of our agreements with you to \<builder's attorney\> for response.

\<He or She\> will handle all future communications and will be in touch with your attorney in the near future.

Sincerely,

[Builder]
cc: \<Builder's attorney\>

5

Customer
Feedback

No one is in a better position to tell you what doing business with your company is like than the people who have done business with your company—from home buyers to real estate agents and trade contractors. This section offers cover letters and surveys of various types—formal and informal—you can use to gather feedback.

One caution, think through your objectives to organize a comprehensive feedback and networking system. A well-planned and efficient program gathers the information you want and avoids annoying customers with too many inquiries.

Evaluating the feedback you obtain from surveys is an art in itself. Discipline yourself to see through emotions to facts and causes. With practice you will be able to see the difference between an isolated problem, perhaps caused by personalities, and a fundamental weakness in your system that requires attention. A timely summary of results, circulated and discussed with company personnel, should lead to actions and improvement.

Written Surveys ➜

Maximize responses to your written surveys by keeping the survey brief—one to four pages. Include specific questions and space for general comments. Request signatures but make them optional.

Expect a 30 to 60 percent rate of return. Including a self-addressed, stamped envelope makes returning the survey more convenient, and therefore you might receive more replies. Mention a requested return date in your cover letter. Ten days is a good time frame.

To achieve higher rates of return, consider implementing a two-part survey system. Because the process of purchasing a home takes several months and includes so many details, send the first questionnaire soon after closing (within 10 days or so) while these events are fresh in the customer's mind.

Conduct the second survey 9 to 14 months after move-in. This questionnaire asks for feedback on design, quality, and warranty service. Asking about these topics soon after closing doesn't give the homeowner time to form opinions. Yet if you wait long enough to ask about design, quality, and service, the customer may have forgotten important points about the process. Hence the need for separate surveys.

Your in-house staff can process customer survey questionnaires like those that follow (Figure 5.1, 5.2, 5.3, and 5.4) or you can have a company that specializes in customer surveys process them. Either way, gather the feedback and act on the results.

FIGURE 5.1 Cover Letter for Post-Closing Survey Questionnaire

\<Date\>
\<Homeowner's Name\>
\<Address\>
\<City, State, and Zip Code\>

Post-Closing Survey Questionnaire

Dear \<Homeowner\>:

Having a new home built is a complicated, exciting, scary, fun, expensive, gratifying, time-consuming, wonderful experience. Many details need to be correct for you to be satisfied with the results. We want to know which of those details we handled well and where we can improve.

Your opinions regarding your home buying experience are valuable to us in this effort. Therefore, we are asking for your feedback.

You will find a survey questionnaire is enclosed. Please take a few minutes to complete and return it to me in the enclosed envelope by \<date\>. A small gift is enclosed as a token of our appreciation for your time.

We look forward to receiving your comments.

Sincerely,

[Builder]
Enclosures

FIGURE 5.2 Post-Closing Survey Questionnaire

Please put a check in the box that most closely describes your opinion. If an item does not apply to you, please check NA, not applicable.

	Excellent	Good	Fair	Poor	NA
Sales Center					
Ease of locating sales center	❏	❏	❏	❏	❏
Sales center's hours convenient	❏	❏	❏	❏	❏
Models clean and well-maintained	❏	❏	❏	❏	❏
[Builder] Sales Counselor					
Interested in my/our needs	❏	❏	❏	❏	❏
Courteous	❏	❏	❏	❏	❏
Knowledgeable about	❏	❏	❏	❏	❏
Product	❏	❏	❏	❏	❏
Options	❏	❏	❏	❏	❏
Procedures	❏	❏	❏	❏	❏
Documents	❏	❏	❏	❏	❏
Volunteered helpful information	❏	❏	❏	❏	❏
Well-organized	❏	❏	❏	❏	❏
Thorough	❏	❏	❏	❏	❏
Reliable	❏	❏	❏	❏	❏
Responded to questions promptly (within 48 hours)	❏	❏	❏	❏	❏
Cooperation/communication with construction	❏	❏	❏	❏	❏
Homeowner Manual					
Format convenient for locating information	❏	❏	❏	❏	❏
Helpfulness of information	❏	❏	❏	❏	❏
Selection Process					
Location and hours clear	❏	❏	❏	❏	❏
Selection staff	❏	❏	❏	❏	❏
Interested in my/our needs	❏	❏	❏	❏	❏
Courteous	❏	❏	❏	❏	❏
Knowledgeable	❏	❏	❏	❏	❏
Volunteered helpful information	❏	❏	❏	❏	❏
Well-organized	❏	❏	❏	❏	❏
Thorough	❏	❏	❏	❏	❏
Reliable	❏	❏	❏	❏	❏
Responded to questions promptly (within 48 hours)	❏	❏	❏	❏	❏
Sufficient range of choices	❏	❏	❏	❏	❏
Pricing clear	❏	❏	❏	❏	❏
Time allotted for making selections sufficient	❏	❏	❏	❏	❏

	Excellent	Good	Fair	Poor	NA
Change order process clear	❏	❏	❏	❏	❏
Change order time limitations reasonable	❏	❏	❏	❏	❏
Overall satisfaction with selections	❏	❏	❏	❏	❏

Preconstruction Conference

	Excellent	Good	Fair	Poor	NA
Sufficient notice prior to meeting	❏	❏	❏	❏	❏
Purpose explained by sales staff	❏	❏	❏	❏	❏
Staff prepared and well-organized	❏	❏	❏	❏	❏
Information presented relevant and useful	❏	❏	❏	❏	❏
Superintendent	❏	❏	❏	❏	❏
Interested in my/our needs	❏	❏	❏	❏	❏
Courteous	❏	❏	❏	❏	❏
Knowledgeable	❏	❏	❏	❏	❏
Volunteered helpful information	❏	❏	❏	❏	❏
Thorough	❏	❏	❏	❏	❏
Reliable	❏	❏	❏	❏	❏
Responded to questions promptly (within 48 hours)	❏	❏	❏	❏	❏

Predrywall Tour

	Excellent	Good	Fair	Poor	NA
Sufficient notice prior to meeting	❏	❏	❏	❏	❏
Purpose explained by sales staff	❏	❏	❏	❏	❏
Home site clean and safe	❏	❏	❏	❏	❏
Information presented relevant and useful	❏	❏	❏	❏	❏
Superintendent responded to questions promptly	❏	❏	❏	❏	❏
Follow-through by superintendent on any items noted	❏	❏	❏	❏	❏

Homeowner Orientation

	Excellent	Good	Fair	Poor	NA
	❏	❏	❏	❏	❏
Sufficient notice prior to the orientation appointment	❏	❏	❏	❏	❏
Purposes of the orientation explained by sales staff	❏	❏	❏	❏	❏
Information presented useful and relevant	❏	❏	❏	❏	❏
Orientation rep	❏	❏	❏	❏	❏
Courteous	❏	❏	❏	❏	❏
Knowledgeable	❏	❏	❏	❏	❏
Volunteered helpful information	❏	❏	❏	❏	❏
Well-organized	❏	❏	❏	❏	❏
Thorough	❏	❏	❏	❏	❏
Reliable	❏	❏	❏	❏	❏
Responded to questions promptly	❏	❏	❏	❏	❏
Overall condition of home at orientation	❏	❏	❏	❏	❏

Closing

	Excellent	Good	Fair	Poor	NA
Sufficient notice prior to the closing appointment	❏	❏	❏	❏	❏
Location and appointment time clear	❏	❏	❏	❏	❏

(continued)

FIGURE 5.2 *(Continued)*

	Excellent	Good	Fair	Poor	NA
Steps for preparation clear (utilities, insurance, final number)	❑	❑	❑	❑	❑
Settlement figures provided for your review 24 hours prior	❑	❑	❑	❑	❑
Closing personnel	❑	❑	❑	❑	❑
Courteous	❑	❑	❑	❑	❑
Well-organized	❑	❑	❑	❑	❑
Documents explained clearly	❑	❑	❑	❑	❑
Thorough	❑	❑	❑	❑	❑

Condition of Your Home at Move-In

	Excellent	Good	Fair	Poor	NA
Complete	❑	❑	❑	❑	❑
Clean	❑	❑	❑	❑	❑
Correct according to selections and change orders	❑	❑	❑	❑	❑
Orientation items completed or scheduled	❑	❑	❑	❑	❑
Satisfaction with orientation item work	❑	❑	❑	❑	❑
Satisfaction with overall condition of the home at move-in	❑	❑	❑	❑	❑

Conclusion

Why did you select us to build your home?

_____

_____

_____

Would you buy from us again?   ❑ Yes   ❑ No   ❑ Undecided

Would you recommend us to others?   ❑ Yes   ❑ No   ❑ With qualifications

What could we have done to make your home buying experience more enjoyable?

_____

_____

_____

Please add any additional comments you would like to share with us.

_____

_____

_____

Optional

_____   _____
Name   Phone

_____
Address

_____
City, State, and Zip Code

Thank you!

FIGURE 5.3 Cover Letter for Year-End Survey

<Date>
<Homeowner's Name>
<Address>
<City, State, Zip Code>

Year-End Survey

Dear <Homeowner>:

Over a year has gone by since you closed on your [Builder] home. We sincerely hope you are enjoying your new home and <Community>.

Now that you have had time to get settled, experience the seasons and holidays, and make use of our warranty service, we once again are asking for your feedback.

Enclosed are a survey questionnaire and return envelope. Please share your opinions with us and return the survey by <date>. Your suggestions are a valuable resource to us in our continuing effort to improve our business.

A gift certificate good for two tickets at <movie theater> are enclosed as our way of saying thank you for your time.

Sincerely,

[Builder]
Enclosures

FIGURE 5.4 Year-End Survey Questionnaire

Please put a check in the box that most closely describes your opinion. If an item does not apply to you, please check NA, not applicable.

	Excellent	Good	Fair	Poor	NA
Design					
Traffic flow convenient	❏	❏	❏	❏	❏
Features appealing and useful	❏	❏	❏	❏	❏
Adequate private areas	❏	❏	❏	❏	❏
Adequate family activity areas	❏	❏	❏	❏	❏
Adequate storage	❏	❏	❏	❏	❏
Value for cost	❏	❏	❏	❏	❏

What would you change about this floor plan? _____
_____
_____

What features would you add? _____
_____
_____

What features would you omit? _____
_____
_____

	Excellent	Good	Fair	Poor	NA
Quality					
Air-conditioning	❏	❏	❏	❏	❏
Appliances	❏	❏	❏	❏	❏
Brick	❏	❏	❏	❏	❏
Cabinets	❏	❏	❏	❏	❏
Carpet	❏	❏	❏	❏	❏
Ceramic tile	❏	❏	❏	❏	❏
Concrete flatwork	❏	❏	❏	❏	❏
Countertops	❏	❏	❏	❏	❏
Doors and locks	❏	❏	❏	❏	❏
Drywall	❏	❏	❏	❏	❏
Electrical	❏	❏	❏	❏	❏
Fireplace	❏	❏	❏	❏	❏
Foundation	❏	❏	❏	❏	❏
Garage overhead door	❏	❏	❏	❏	❏
Hardware	❏	❏	❏	❏	❏
Hardwood floors	❏	❏	❏	❏	❏
Heating system	❏	❏	❏	❏	❏
Insulation	❏	❏	❏	❏	❏
Landscaping	❏	❏	❏	❏	❏
Paint and stain	❏	❏	❏	❏	❏
Plumbing	❏	❏	❏	❏	❏
Resilient flooring	❏	❏	❏	❏	❏
Roof	❏	❏	❏	❏	❏
Rough carpentry	❏	❏	❏	❏	❏

	Excellent	Good	Fair	Poor	NA
Siding	❏	❏	❏	❏	❏
Stucco	❏	❏	❏	❏	❏
Water heater	❏	❏	❏	❏	❏
Windows, screens, patio doors	❏	❏	❏	❏	❏
Wood trim	❏	❏	❏	❏	❏

Warranty Service

	Excellent	Good	Fair	Poor	NA
Standards clear	❏	❏	❏	❏	❏
Procedures clear	❏	❏	❏	❏	❏
Procedures convenient	❏	❏	❏	❏	❏
Warranty decisions reasonable	❏	❏	❏	❏	❏
Warranty repairs explained	❏	❏	❏	❏	❏
Repair work quality					
Service orders completed in 10 business days	❏	❏	❏	❏	❏
Communications regarding back ordered item	❏	❏	❏	❏	❏
Clean up of work area	❏	❏	❏	❏	❏
Builder warranty staff	❏	❏	❏	❏	❏
Trade contractor personnel	❏	❏	❏	❏	❏

Would you buy from us again?   ❏ Yes   ❏ No   ❏ Undecided

Would you recommend us to others?   ❏ Yes   ❏ No   ❏ With qualifications

_____
_____
_____

What could we have done to make your home buying experience more enjoyable?____
_____
_____
_____

Please add any additional comments you would like to share with us._____
_____
_____
_____

Optional

_____
Name   Phone

_____
Address

_____
City, State and Zip Code

Thank you!

Postcard Surveys ➜

Some builders use a quick postcard survey after each phase of the process: contract, mortgage application, selections, preconstruction conference, frame-stage tour, orientation, closing, and warranty visits. Self-addressed, postage-paid postcards similar to those that follow can be handed or mailed to customers. If a customer is dissatisfied with something, the sooner you find out about it the better your chance of restoring goodwill. Figures 5.5 through 5.10 show several examples.

Note that the maximum postcard size is 6 inches long, 4¼ inches high, and 0.016 inches thick. If any dimension is larger, you need to use the first-class rate. For some purposes, in the interest of speed, you might want to use first-class postage even though your postcard meets the size standards.

FIGURE 5.5 Postcard Survey Questionnaire—Lender

[Date]

Dear _____ :

Home buyer feedback about the services provided by area lenders helps us know which organizations to suggest to buyers. Please respond to the items below and mail this card.

Lender	Yes	No	Comment
Set the loan application appointment promptly	❏	❏	_____
Explained financing options available	❏	❏	_____
Completed the application efficiently	❏	❏	_____
Provided weekly updates on your application	❏	❏	_____
Responded to questions within one business day	❏	❏	_____
Followed through to obtain final approval	❏	❏	_____

Additional remarks _____

_____

_____

_____   _____
Signature   Date

FIGURE 5.6 Postcard Survey Questionnaire—Selections

[Date]

Dear _____ :

After completing the selection decision for your new home, please give us your feedback
about that process and the service we provided by responding to the items listed below
and mailing this card.

	Yes	No	Comment
Selection staff prepared	❑	❑	_____
Knowledgeable	❑	❑	_____
Well-organized	❑	❑	_____
Thorough	❑	❑	_____
Reliable	❑	❑	_____
Answered questions promptly	❑	❑	_____
Adequate range of choice	❑	❑	_____
Pricing clear	❑	❑	_____
Sufficient time allotted	❑	❑	_____

Additional remarks _____

_____

_____   _____
Signature   Date

FIGURE 5.7 Postcard Survey Questionnaire—Preconstruction Conference

[Date]

Dear _____:

We offer the preconstruction conference to review your decisions about your home and provide you with an overview of the upcoming construction process. Please evaluate our success by responding to the topics listed below and mailing this card.

	Yes	No	Comment
Staff prepared and well-organized	❏	❏	_____
Information presented relevant and useful	❏	❏	_____
Superintendent			
Interested in my/our needs	❏	❏	_____
Courteous	❏	❏	_____
Knowledgeable	❏	❏	_____
Volunteered helpful information	❏	❏	_____
Thorough	❏	❏	_____
Reliable	❏	❏	_____
Responded to questions promptly	❏	❏	_____

_____   _____
Signature   Date

FIGURE 5.8 Postcard Survey Questionnaire—Predrywall Tour

[Date]

Dear _____:

Please share your opinion about your predrywall tour. Our goals were to answer your questions, give you an opportunity to see the quality inside the walls of your new home, and confirm that changes you ordered have been correctly installed. Your feedback helps us to improve our systems and procedures.

	Yes	No	Comment
Homesite clean and safe	❏	❏	_____
Information presented relevant and useful	❏	❏	_____
Superintendent responded to questions promptly	❏	❏	_____
Superintendent followed through on items noted	❏	❏	_____

Additional remarks _____

_____

_____

_____

_____   _____
Signature   Date

FIGURE 5.9 Postcard Survey Questionnaire—Orientation

[Date]

Dear _____:

Following your homeowner orientation please take a few moments to respond to the items below and mail this card to our office. Your feedback helps us improve our systems and procedures.

	Yes	No	Comment
Staff prepared and well-organized	❏	❏	_____
Information presented relevant and useful	❏	❏	_____
Orientation representative	❏	❏	_____
Courteous	❏	❏	_____
Knowledgeable	❏	❏	_____
Volunteered helpful information	❏	❏	_____
Thorough	❏	❏	_____
Reliable	❏	❏	_____
Responded to questions promptly	❏	❏	_____
Satisfied with overall condition of home at orientation	❏	❏	_____

Additional remarks _____

_____

_____   _____

Signature   Date

FIGURE 5.10 Postcard Survey Questionnaire—Warranty Service

[Date]

Dear _____:

The work order listed below should be completed within 10 workdays. Your feedback on this work is valuable to us in assessing our staff and improving our service. Please take a moment to share your comments with us.

Service Order No. _____ Issued to _____

	Yes	No	Comment
Contacted promptly	❑	❑	_____
Courteous, knowledgeable	❑	❑	_____
Good quality workmanship	❑	❑	_____
Cleaned up after completion	❑	❑	_____

Additional remarks _____

_____

_____

_____

_____   _____
Signature   Date

Phone Survey Announcement ➜

Another method of obtaining customer feedback is to conduct phone surveys. Like written surveys, you can have in-house personnel or an outside firm do these surveys. An advantage to this approach is that the interviewer can ask follow-up questions to clarify points a customer makes. A disadvantage is that the interviewer's personality can influence the answers.

To maximize success with this method, announce the upcoming phone survey a few days prior to homeowners receiving the call. The letter in figure 5.11 shows one way to do this.

FIGURE 5.11 Phone Survey Announcement

\<Date\>
\<Homeowner's Name\>
\<Address\>
\<City, State, and Zip Code\>

Phone Survey Announcement

Dear \<Homeowner\>:

May we ask for a few minutes of your time? Within the next several days \<name of interviewer or company\> will call you to conduct a brief telephone survey about your new home buying experience.

These conversations usually take from 7 to 10 minutes. As a thank you for your participation, you will receive \<gift\> in the mail a few days after your interview.

We look forward to receiving your feedback and hope you will be available to participate.

Sincerely,

[Builder]
cc: \<Interviewer or company\>

Focus Group ➔

The impact of a focus group is different from the impact of surveys. The live answers and immediacy of these discussions makes service issues vivid. While they do not collect the views of as large a number of people as a written survey can, they are a source of feedback that is inexpensive, quick, and potent. Figures 5.12 through 5.14 provide invitation, confirmation, and thank-you-for-participating letters. The sidebar offers some hints to consider in your planning.

As with written surveys, the effectiveness of focus groups depends on what you do with the results. Summarize notes from the meeting, then circulate and discuss them with your staff. Whether you identify one idea or a list of improvements for your customer service program, you will find the focus group approach to be worth the time and effort.

Focus Group Hints

- Keep the group small so everyone has a chance to speak. Invite a few more people than you expect to end up with. A good target number is 12 to 16 participants.
- Saturdays are popular for these sessions with Thursday evening a second choice.
- Two hours seem to be a good time frame. Include a short break.
- Serve light refreshments.
- Appoint a neutral facilitator who can keep the discussion on track.
- Appoint someone else to take notes.
- Have a planned agenda of several key questions. Keep the topics short and clear. You might want to zero in on one aspect of your process, such as selections, or perhaps you will want comments on the entire experience.
- Remember that this time is your customers' opportunity to tell you what they think. Avoid explanations, just listen, and absorb what they have to say.
- Conduct a debriefing with your staff after the focus group to report on the results and target new improvements.
- Remember that expenses for a focus group can vary considerably depending on whether and what kind of refreshments you provide, where it takes place, the gifts given to the participants, and who facilitates the discussion (an outsider, a staff member, or the builder).

FIGURE 5.12 Invitation to Focus Group

<Date>
<Homeowner's Name>
<Address>
<City, State, and Zip Code>

Focus Group Invitation

Dear <Homeowner>:

As part of an ongoing effort to understand the desires and needs of our customers, we conduct several focus groups each year.

We hope you will join your neighbors at the next focus group scheduled for <Community>. It will be take place—

<time>, <date>
<location>

Please attend and share feedback about the homebuilding process, and our procedures and services. Light refreshments will be served.

Please RSVP to <name> at <phone>. We look forward to hearing from you.

If you have any questions, please contact me.

Sincerely,

[Builder]

FIGURE 5.13 **Confirmation of Focus Group Participation**

\<Date\>
\<Homeowner's Name\>
\<Address\>
\<City, State, and Zip Code\>

Focus Group Confirmation

Dear \<Homeowner\>:

Thank you for agreeing to participate in the \<Community\> focus group scheduled for—

\<time\>, \<date\>
\<location\>

We look forward to seeing you and hearing your comments.

If you have any questions, please contact me.

Sincerely,

[Builder]

FIGURE 5.14 Thank You for Participating

\<Date>
\<Homeowner's Name>
\<Address>
\<City, State, and Zip Code>

Thank You

Dear \<Homeowner>:

Because of homeowners like you, the \<Community> focus group held on \<date> was enjoyable and productive. We gathered valuable ideas and are busy putting your feedback to work.

We appreciate your time and effort and hope you will enjoy the enclosed thank you gift.

If you have any questions, please contact me.

Sincerely,

[Builder]
Enclosure

Survey of Real Estate Agents ➜

A healthy relationship with local real estate agents is essential to the long-term success of builders in most regions. These relationships are too easily taken for granted or left to chance.

Check on your reputation with the real estate community with a quick and easy survey such as the one in Figure 5.15. Real estate agents are unlikely to complete a long survey because

For more information on developing productive relationships with real estate agents in your region, see *Sales Management Tool Kit* by Dennis Radice.[5]

of their busy schedules. Correct any conditions the surveys bring to your attention. The fact that you cared enough to ask will make a good impression.

FIGURE 5.15 Survey Questionnaire for Real Estate Agents

<Date>

<Real Estate Agent's Name>
<Real Estate Brokerage or Company>
<Street Address>
<City, State, and Zip>

Re: <Home Buyer's Name>, <Community>, <closing date>

Dear <Real Estate Agent's Name>:

We would like your opinion. We are sincerely interested in your comments regarding our product and service. Please take a few minutes to complete the questions listed below and return this sheet in the enclosed self-addressed, stamped envelope.

1. Please check the reasons you selected our product to show to your client.
   ❑ Reputation ❑ Client's request ❑ Construction quality ❑ Location
   ❑ Financing ❑ Neighborhood ❑ Benefits, features, appliances ❑ Price
   ❑ Size ❑ Another agent ❑ Options and upgrades ❑ Design
   ❑ Other

2. Were you greeted in a warm and professional manner on each visit to our sales center?
   ❑ Yes ❑ No

3. Was our company and product line accurately described and presented in a helpful way? ❑ Yes ❑ No

4. Were your or your client's concerns addressed quickly and effectively? ❑ Yes ❑ No

5. Please rate the items listed below:

	Highly Satisfied	Satisfied	Mildly Dissatisfied	Highly Dissatisfied	NA
Sales personnel					
Floor plans					
Quality					
Orientation					
Warranty service					

6. Would you recommend us to others? ❑ Yes ❑ No ❑ Undecided

7. Please add any other comments about our company, product, personnel, or service.

_____

Name   Company

Your feedback is most valuable to us in improving our product and service.

Thank you!

[Builder]

Trade Contractor Survey ➡

Your trade contractors represent a wealth of knowledge and serve as a valuable resource. Requesting feedback from trade contractors with a survey such as the one shown in Figure 5.16 can gather useful information and focus your attention on opportunities for improvement. Trade contractors may suggest improved methods and materials or help you identify procedures that need updating. Ask for and listen to their opinions and ideas.

FIGURE 5.16 **Trade Contractor Survey Questionnaire**

We need your opinion. We are sincerely interested in your comments regarding both our product and service. Please take a few minutes to complete the questions below and return this sheet in the enclosed self-addressed, stamped envelope.

	Yes	No
1. Are the construction standards and specifications you are expected to meet clear and complete?	❏	❏
2. Are these standards and specifications consistently and fairly enforced?	❏	❏
3. Is adequate notice provided regarding routine scheduling of your work?	❏	❏
4. Is adequate notice provided regarding customer-approved changes from normal plans?	❏	❏
5. Are our homes ready for your work when you arrive on the job?	❏	❏
6. Are clean-up procedures clear and enforced?	❏	❏
7. Are safety practices in place and enforced?	❏	❏
8. Do customers interfere with the progress of your efforts?	❏	❏
9. Is supervision adequate, allowing you an opportunity to ask questions and obtain quick and accurate answers?	❏	❏
10. Are your invoices or draws processed efficiently and payments made on time?	❏	❏
11. Are warranty standards and procedures clear and fairly enforced?	❏	❏
12. Can we do anything to assist you or to provide better service to our customers?	❏	❏

Please add any other comments about our company, methods, product, personnel, or service. Include any suggestions you have to improve our product, and to save time, money, or effort.

_____

_____

_____

_____

_____

Thank you! Your feedback is most valuable to us in improving our product and service. Your signature is requested but not required.

_____   _____   _____
Name   Company   Date

Selected Bibliography

Jaffe, David. *Contracts and Liability*, 4th ed. Washington, D.C.: Home Builder Press, National Association of Home Builders, 1996.

Martin, Judith. *Miss Manners' Basic Training: Communication*. New York: Crown Publishers, Inc., 1997.

Popcorn, Faith, and Lys Marigold. *Clicking*. New York: Harper Collins Publishers, 1996.

Radice, Dennis. *Sales Management Tool Kit*. Washington, D.C.: Home Builder Press, National Association of Home Builders, 2000.

Roddick, Ellen. *Writing that Means Business: A Manager's Guide*. New York: MacMillan Publishing Company, 1984.

Smith, Carol. *Customer Relations Handbook for Builders*. Washington, D.C.: Home Builder Press, National Association of Home Builders, 1998.

_____. *Homeowner Manual: A Model for Home Builders*. Washington, D.C.: Home Builder Press, National Association of Home Builders, 1997.

Notes

1. Ellen Roddick, *Writing that Means Business: A Manager's Guide.* (New York: MacMillan Publishing Company, 1984).
2. Judith Martin, *Miss Manners' Basic Training: Communication.* (New York: Crown Publishers, Inc., 1997).
3. Carol Smith, *Homeowner Manual: A Model for Home Builders* (Washington, D.C.: Home Builder Press, National Association of Home Builders, 1997).
4. For more information on completion dates see David Jaffe, "Time of Commencement and Substantial Completion," Chapter 2, Contract Between Builder and Buyer or Owner, p. 12, *Contracts and Liability for Builders and Remodelers*, 4th ed. (Washington, D.C.; Home Builder Press, National Association of Home Builders, 1996); for more information on excusable delays see Liquidated Damages and Unavoidable Delay," also in Jaffe, p. 17.
5. *Moving into Your New Home*, The Builder Brochure Series (Washington, D.C.: Home Builder Press, National Association of Home Builders, 1999). To learn about other brochures in the Builder Brochure Series contact (800) 223–2665.
6. David Jaffe, *Warranties and Disclaimers for Builders* (Washington, D.C.: Home Builder Press, National Association of Home Builders, 1999).
7. Dennis Radice, *Sales Management Tool Kit* (Washington, D.C.: Home Builder Press, National Association of Home Builders, 2000).
8. David Jaffe, *Contracts and Liability for Builders and Remodelers* 4th ed. (Washington, D.C.: Home Builder Press, National Association of Home Builders, 1996), p. 28.
9. Carol Smith, *Customer Relations Handbook for Builders* (Washington, D.C.: Home Builder Press, National Association of Home Builders, 1998).
10. "3. Covered Defect," "Figure 3.1, Sample One-Year Limited Warranty Agreement," *Customer Service Handbook*, Vol. II (Washington, D.C.: Home Builder Press, National Association of Home Builders, 1998), p. 29.
11. Susan Edwards, *Dangerous Clients: How to Protect Yourself* (San Francisco: Miller Freeman Books, 1998).